MADRID
—in your pocket—

MICHELIN®

MAIN CONTRIBUTOR: JACK ALTMAN

PHOTOGRAPH CREDITS
Photos supplied by The Travel Library: A Amsel 12,
18, 28-29, 36 (left, right), 44, 51, 64, 65, 68, 109, 115;
Stuart Black front cover, back cover, title page, 7, 9, 21,
23, 24, 27, 30, 31, 32, 34, 35, 37, 38, 41, 42, 45, 46, 47,
48 (top, bottom), 50, 52, 53, 59, 61, 62, 63, 66 (top,
bottom), 67, 69, 70, 75, 76, 78, 82, 83, 84, 87, 89, 91,
94, 96, 99, 100, 102, 104, 105, 106, 107, 111, 117, 120,
125; Philip Enticknap 5, 10, 11, 33, 39, 81, 88, 92;
R Richardson 85, 113, 123; Gino Russo 72.
Other photos: Prado, Madrid/The Bridgeman Art
Library 54, 55, 57; Giraudon/The Bridgeman Art
Library 60.

Front cover: café scene, Plaza Mayor; back cover:
tapas bar; title page; statue of Philip III

MANUFACTURE FRANÇAISE DES PNEUMATIQUES MICHELIN

Société en commandite par actions au capital de 2 000 000 000 de francs

Place des Carmes-Déchaux – 63 Clermont-Ferrand (France)

R.C.S. Clermont-Fd 855 200 507

© Michelin et Cie. Propriétaires-Éditeurs 1997

Dêpôt légal Mai 97 – ISBN 2-06-651201-X – ISSN en cours

Printed in Spain 4-97

CONTENTS

INTRODUCTION

The monument to Alfonso XII is an imposing backdrop to the lake at Retiro Park.

In the last quarter of the 20C, Madrid has emerged as a capital whose dynamic cultural and social life bears honourable comparison with any of its older European rivals. More than the vision of its rulers, this has been the achievement of the town's artists, musicians, film-makers, fashion designers and, above all, the citizens themselves. As an improbable, even artificial, latecomer among European capitals, established only in 1561, what it may lack in spectacular architectural landmarks, the city makes up in its present-day ambience of boisterous modernity.

To achieve its new vibrancy, the city had to remove cold, hard layers of political calculation left by Philip II, who wanted a capital in the middle of the country without regional attachments, and by General Franco, who made it the chief focus of his dictatorship. Things have calmed down since the hottest days of the post-Franco *Movida* cultural movement, but the bars of the Chueca and Malasaña neighbourhoods still bounce all night. Gentler folk stick to the *tapas* bars *(tascas)* and cafés around the elegant Plaza Mayor and Santa Ana, but the scene is just as lively.

Not that higher cultural demands are neglected. Madrileños take pride in the golden triangle formed by the Prado with its Velázquez, El Greco and Goya treasures, the Thyssen-Bornemisza's awesome private collection and the Reina Sofía modern art centre displaying Picasso's *Guernica*. And the city's central location makes the architectural jewels of Toledo, Segovia and Philip II's Escorial Palace, or the royal gardens at Aranjuez, all easily accessible.

GEOGRAPHY

Corresponding precisely to the needs of Philip II when he chose it as his capital, the city stands at the geographical centre of Spain, equidistantly 300km (187.5 miles) from the Mediterranean to the east and the Atlantic to the north. Madrid's altitude of 646m (2 120ft) above sea level makes it the highest capital in Europe. Sitting on the peninsula's vast, open, arid Meseta plateau, with the modest Manzanares river flowing to the west of the city, it enjoys a dry continental climate of extremes, with very hot summers and very cold winters.

An oft-repeated proverb dating back to the Renaissance says, with a little exaggeration, *'Madrid, nueve meses de invierno, tres meses de infierno'* (Madrid, nine months of winter, three months of hell). In August the temperature averages 30°C (86°F), while in winter it can fall several degrees below zero. The summers are, above all, very dry, and dust brought in from the surrounding Meseta has to be laid to rest each night by municipal workers hosing down the city's streets.

The city proper has a population of nearly 3 million, and covers an area of 531 sq km (205 sq miles). The Communidad de Madrid (the Madrid region) extends north to the Sierra de Guadarrama and south to Aranjuez on the Río Tajo (Tagus river). It encompasses a total area of 7 995 sq km (3 086 sq miles) and adds another 2 000 000 inhabitants. Population drift will continue to favour this region over the metropolis as the

The Sierra de Guadarrama marks the northernmost extent of the Madrid region.

more prosperous bourgeoisie moves to the suburbs north-west of the city around El Escorial, while the working classes migrate south and east.

Dotted with earth-hued villages, the plateau's endless horizons are covered with fields of wheat, olive groves and vineyards. The Guadarrama and Gredos ranges provide a mountain barrier to the north and west, rarely rising above 2 000m (6 562ft) but high enough for some serious skiing in winter, with the highest peak reaching 2 430m (7 972ft).

Inside the city, it is four man-made landmarks rather than geographical features that provide easy orientation: west of the city centre is the Royal Palace; on the east side is the Buen Retiro Park; to the north stands the AZCA district's Picasso Tower and Bilbao/Vizcaya Tower; and, at the very centre, is the clocktower of Puerta del Sol.

HISTORY

Much as its champions would like otherwise, Madrid is not an ancient city. The earliest evidence of human presence in the area is some bones found on the city's eastern outskirts dating to around 3000 BC. Later the Roman conquerors of the 2C BC encountered Celto-Iberian hunters and herdsmen on the Meseta plateau and founded towns at Toledo and Alcalá de Henares, but no evidence of a human settlement on the site of Madrid has been found.

Visigoths and Moors
When Spain's Visigoth rulers, not at all 'barbarian' but Romanized Christians, arrived from the Danube Valley in the 5C,

they established their capital at Toledo.

Even by the time of the Moorish (Arab and Berber) conquest of 711, Madrid was still little more than a hamlet and did not begin to grow until **Emir Mohammed I** built a fortress *(alcázar)* there in around 875. The walled town that grew up for the Muslim, Jewish and Christian population drew its modern name from the Arabs' fortress, Majrit, which was named after the small streams in the settlement.

In 1469, King Ferdinand II of Aragon married Isabel of Castilla, uniting the two great kingdoms of Spain.

Christian Reconquest

Over the next 200 years, the town was subject to constant raids by Christian kings on their way to Toledo. **Alfonso VI** finally took Madrid in 1083, with 200 cavalry and 500 infantry.

The city's loyalty in the Reconquista campaign was rewarded with the control of the mountains, pastures and hamlets between Madrid and Segovia. By 1346, the first real Town Hall *(ayuntamiento)* was established in the San Salvador cloister that is now Plaza de la Villa, and the bustling area around Calle Mayor, site of the Arabs' bazaar, became the focus for shops, brothels and gambling dens.

In 1390, **Henry III** launched Madrid's first campaign against the Jews. Their houses were

FERNANDO EL CATOLICO

plundered, and they were forced to wear distinctive signs of their religion.

From 1480, the Spanish Inquisition's tribunal in Toledo decided on the trial and execution of many of Madrid's Jews, Muslims and other 'heretics'. Jews were expelled from Spain in 1492, in the campaign to achieve *limpieza de sangre* (Christian blood-purity).

Becoming the Nation's Capital

Madrid's civic prestige rose as it was regularly chosen for meetings of the Cortes (parliament) and for the formal proclamation of King Charles I of Spain, in 1516. The future Habsburg emperor, **Charles V**, rebuilt the Alcázar and his son, **Philip II**, transferred the royal capital from Toledo to Madrid in June 1561.

At this time, Madrid's population was little more than 15 000, while wealthy, tradition-laden Toledo numbered over 70 000, but in a land of fiercely rival regions Madrid had the appeal of neutrality; it was also geographically central. More important, political power would now be separate from the church authority of Toledo. Philip emphasized the desire to keep his own counsel by building a retreat at El Escorial palace and monastery.

While these aptly austere edifices were being completed outside of the town, the monastery of San Jerónimo east of the city centre served as the pious king's retreat, the *buen retiro* that gave its name to Madrid's best-loved park.

Philip II (1527–1598) moved the capital of Spain from Toledo to Madrid.

Madrid of the Habsburgs

In striking contrast to the splendour of the Spanish Empire, Madrid remained architecturally unimpressive, with few of the Renaissance and baroque monuments that graced Europe's other capitals. With Philip's energies focussed on creating El Escorial, the city itself had no cathedral, university and few grandiose buildings. An exception is the arcaded Plaza Mayor, laid out in 1619 for royal processions, bullfights – and the Inquisition's trials and executions.

The Habsburg rulers made up for the lack of architectural grandeur with the splendour of their art collections – Flemish, Italian and native Spanish. **Philip IV** (1621–1665) was particularly active in encouraging Spain's

Pietro Tacca's equestrian statue of Philip IV adorns the Plaza de Oriente.

finest artists and writers. **Velázquez** and **Zurbarán** were both court painters; poet and playwright **Lope de Vega** was born in Madrid; and **Miguel de Cervantes** published the first part of *Don Quixote* in 1605 (completed ten years later) in the capital.

Under the French Bourbons

After a series of economic, diplomatic and military disasters, the 17C ended with the extinction of Madrid's Habsburg dynasty. The heirless Charles II chose as his successor Louis XIV's Bourbon grandson, **Philip V** (1700–46). Arch-conservative Carlists, supporting the rival claim of Austrian archduke Charles of Habsburg, subjected Madrid to a series of military occupations until a treaty secured Philip V's position in 1713.

Disappointed at not getting the French

Affectionately known as the 'mayor-king', Charles III left his mark on Madrid with the improvements he instigated.

throne, Philip V never took to Madrid, preferring the miniature Versailles he built at La Granja de San Ildefonso, between Madrid and Segovia. Replacing the alcázar destroyed by fire in 1734, Madrid's new Royal Palace put a neo-classical stamp on the city's architecture. Silks, laces and brocade, powdered wigs and other French frivolities replaced the stiff formality of Habsburg court dress.

Honouring him with the triumphal arch of Puerta de Alcalá (1778) and an equestrian statue on the Puerta del Sol (1994), Madrid regards King **Charles III** (1759–88) as the best mayor it ever had. The son of Philip V (by his second marriage), Charles paved the streets, improved the sanitation, put in street-lighting, extended the popular *paseo* promenades and planted more trees. In 1785 the Prado was opened, initially for the natural sciences but converted to a museum for the royal art collections 30 years later.

The 19C

Facing dangerous libertarian ideas filtering across the Pyrenees from the French Revolution, Madrid's rulers imposed censorship and gave renewed support to the Inquisition. The French invasion of 1808 did not improve matters, even after Napoleon replaced the heavy-handed **Joachim Murat** with his brother **Joseph Bonaparte**. On 2 May, riots against the French occupying force broke out in Madrid. The armed insurrection was crushed by a French force of 30 000 troops. In his paintings *Dos de Mayo* and *Tres de Mayo*, **Goya** immortalized the street battles and executions which left 450 dead. In an attempt at enlightened government, Joseph Bonaparte banished the Inquisition, encouraged literary cafés and demolished several churches and monasteries to make way for new city squares.

After the British drove out the French in 1814, the Spanish regime of **Ferdinand VII** proved more repressive than ever, abolishing the Constitution and dissolving the Cortes. Discord throughout the country continued, and not until the signing of the Constitution in 1876 was there peace in Madrid.

Civil War

In 1917, while the Bolshevik revolution was erupting on the other side of Europe, the army in Madrid repressed a general strike led by Spain's Socialist Worker's Party, formed some 40 years earlier. The city was ripe for the populist dictatorship of **General Primo de Rivera** (1923–30) and expanded under his large-scale industrialization programme. But in 1931, municipal elections brought left-wing government to Madrid, soon followed by a **Republican** victory at national level.

Amid church calls for a return to 'throne and altar', the city was caught up in a violent spiral of right-wing provocations by the fascist Falange party, leftist anti-clerical action and political assassinations on both sides. After a left-wing Popular Front coalition came to power in 1936, the murder in Madrid of a Socialist army officer and the reprisal killing of right-wing politician Calvo Sotelo led to all-out civil war. Anti-Republican troops led by **General Francisco Franco** surrounded the capital. Faced with the Republican forces' strong resistance, Franco launched a prolonged siege and called in aerial bombardment by units of

Mussolini's Italian air force, shelling university buildings, libraries, theatres and cinemas.

The three-year resistance of Madrid citizens became a symbol of the national struggle for democracy, but Franco's army, backed by superior Italian and German firepower, finally marched into the city on 28 March 1939. On the Paseo de la Castellana, the devout Franco, calling himself *'caudillo por la gracia de Dios'* (leader by the grace of God), called on the people to observe order, religion and absolute submission to the principles of his *Movimiento*. Over the next decade, in constant fear of 'godless Communists and Free Masons' Franco had, by the account of his own historians, at least 30 000 regime opponents executed, many more according to other sources.

From Franco to Movida

Spain's ties with the German-Italian Axis disqualified it from Marshall Plan aid, delaying Madrid's economic recovery from the devastating civil war until the 1950s. Prevailing influence in Franco's government was the Catholic **Opus Dei** movement (founded in Madrid in 1935 and blessed by Pope Pius XI in 1947), preaching a morally rigid form of modern capitalism. Puritanical censorship of films, books and newspapers was accompanied by Madrid's first skyscrapers and a glut of new cars in the city centre. Despite fears of immoral foreign contagion, Franco bowed to his Opus Dei economic experts' advice in opening the floodgates to mass tourism (one million in 1951, 16 million by 1965 and 60 million today).

Foreign 'contagion' was a reality, if only slight. In 1968, when revolt swept through Paris, Berlin and Chicago, the university of Madrid staged a fundraising concert by protest-singer Raimon for striking workers in the city suburbs. Franco felt secure. The next year, he named Juan Carlos de Borbón to succeed him as head of state, certain he would acquiesce in the Franquist policies of his prime minister, Carrero Blanco. 'Everything is tied up,' said Franco, 'and nicely tied up' *(Todo está atado y bien atado)*.

In 1973, Carrero Blanco was killed by ETA Basque extremists, who then launched a murderous attack on police chiefs in a Puerta del Sol café. At a last mass meeting in Madrid in October, 1975, the gravely ill Franco condemned 'an internationally orchestrated leftist Masonic plot', and died a month later.

After a prudent period of transition, **King Juan Carlos** replaced Franco's prime minister, Arias Navarro, with the moderate conservative, Adolfo Suárez. A new democratic constitution was proclaimed and censorship halted, but the economy, overheated by years of forced growth, went into recession.

In its first municipal elections since 1931, Madrid chose in 1979 a Socialist-Communist coalition headed by **Enrique Tierno Galván**. This forward-looking philosopher, revered by the young as *el viejo profesor*, 'the old professor', became the Mayor of the *Movida*, a slang word for the new mobile spirit of creativity in post-Franco Spain, spearheaded by Madrid. Tierno Galván reintroduced the carnival and neighbourhood festivities banned under the prudish old regime. The lifelong Marxist encouraged churches to ring their bells as never before, opened new libraries and cultural centres, and brought ducks and carp to swim in the newly cleaned Manzanares river.

In 1981, die-hard Franquists made a last farcical effort to turn the clock back when Colonel Antonio Tejero tried to hold up parliament, firing shots into the ceiling of the Cortes and shouting *'Nadie se mueva!'* – 'Nobody moves!' The putsch failed and a million Madrileños demonstrated in the streets, shouting: 'Everybody moves!' Many say that the *Movida* has ended, others that it has now evolved into the city's way of life, with the slogan: 'Everybody moves!'

THE PEOPLE AND CULTURE

For centuries, the Madrileños had a reputation for being austere. It reflected the heavy influence of the town's authoritarian rulers – 400 years apart – Philip II and Franco. In today's more liberal atmosphere, the people give vent to feelings that seem to mirror the extremes of their climate. Young or old, they can be astonishingly exuberant, partying till all hours of the night, but can descend to the depths of bluest melancholy – at the same party.

Madrileños do not like half measures. The same awesome fervour that the city's devout Catholics bring to Sunday mass, albeit in dwindling numbers, is there among pagan revellers at the *discobares*, the neo-flamenco clubs and the bullfights at Las Ventas.

There is also a new vehemence to the political and philosophical arguments conducted in literary cafés and *tapas* bars (*tascas*) in the post-Franco era. Equally extravagant are the street-fashions favoured

by the young – and the not-so-young making up for lost time – setting Madrid uninhibitedly apart from the more sophisticated, traditional styles of Paris or Rome.

Traditional dancing in the Plaza Mayor.

But not all is excess: ambulant *tuna* musicians strike a gentler note in *mesones* taverns, paying for their university studies with their guitars. And nothing could be more serene and dignified than the Madrileño bourgeoisie taking their evening stroll on the Paseo del Prado or Castellana.

Architecture

The demolitions of the Christian Reconquista, fires, wars and – most devastating of all – urban redevelopment in the 19C and 20C, have left little architectural trace of the city's Moorish beginnings. A piece of wall from the Moorish Alcázar fortress destroyed by fire in 1734 is to be found south of the cathedral. Even the **Mudéjar** architecture, a Moorish-inspired style combining brick and *azulejos* (enamelled ceramic tiles), survives only in three towers: the churches of San Nicolás (12C) and San Piedro el Viejo (1354) and the Torre de los Lujanes (Lujan Tower), a 15C prison across from the Town Hall.

Juan de Herrera, greatest of Spain's **Renaissance** architects, built his most important monument just outside Madrid: Philip II's solemn El Escorial palace and monastery. With the destruction of Herrera's work on the capital's Alcázar, the only Renaissance buildings to survive are the elegant Casa de Cisneros, the convent of Descalzas Reales and Segovia Bridge.

The city's great **baroque** monument is the beautifully laid out Plaza Mayor, an Italian-style piazza designed by **Juan Gómez de Mora** in keeping with the tastes of Spain's Neapolitan-educated monarchs. This Italian baroque influence is also evident in the oval-domed church of San Miguel. Madrid-born **José Benito Churriguera** gave his name to an extravagantly ornate baroque style (Churrigueresque) that has notably survived in the façade of the Municipal Museum.

The **neo-classical** style preferred by the French Bourbon and exemplified in the Royal Palace became the predominant style of museums, churches and government buildings. Otherwise, the 20C urban landscape is dominated by the highrise towers of the Franco era's building boom, most successfully the Torres Blancas (White Towers) of **Sáenz de Oiza**. Madrid's post-Franco era is characterized by its tallest building, the 45-storey Torre Picasso (Picasso Tower) by **Minoru Yamasaki** (1989), and the **post-modern** style of its new museums, its bars and its cafés.

The great Velázquez greets visitors to the Prado.

Arts and Letters

Paradoxically, Madrid's golden age in painting and literature accompanied the Spanish Empire's dramatic decline in the 17C. The transfer of the capital in the previous century from church-dominated Toledo to Madrid was paralleled by a similar transition in painting. The ecstatic religious works of Greek-born Domenikos Theotokopoulos, known as **El Greco**, gave way to the more worldly humanity of **Velázquez** (1599–1660). Born in Seville, Diego Rodríguez de Silva y Velázquez moved to Madrid in 1623 and quickly became court painter under the patronage of Count de Olivares. The painter's profound and subtle intelligence enabled him to serve his royal masters, Philip IV and Don Carlos, with portraits and battle scenes that somehow satisfied their self-esteem while uncompromisingly revealing their physical and psychological frailties. He brought the same insights to the more earthy subjects of drunkards and dwarfs, with his matchless technique, drawing on observation of Flemish and Italian masters.

The prince of Spanish painters undoubtedly influenced his fellow Sevillan **Zurbarán** (1598–1664). The latter's visits to

Madrid imbued his religious subjects, particularly portraits of Franciscan monks, with a striking simplicity and realism remote from the emotional religiosity of El Greco. The Neapolitan painter, **Luca Giordano** (1634–1705), worked for ten years at the court of Charles II, both in Madrid and at El Escorial, leaving his mark on Spanish painting with virtuoso frescoes of biblical and mythological subjects and monumental battle scenes.

Among Madrid's many brilliant playwrights in this golden era were **Tirso de Molina**, famous for creating the greatest of all lovers, Don Juan, and **Calderón de la Barca**, who wrote both cloak-and-dagger and philosophical plays. But the undisputed founding father of Spanish theatre was **Lope de Vega** (1562–1635), poet, wit, notorious womanizer and soldier in the Spanish Armada. Born in Madrid of peasant stock, he delighted Madrid audiences with his common touch, breaking down the barriers of comedy and tragedy. His plays are estimated to number between 1 500 and 1 800, of which 470 have survived.

Giant among novelists, **Miguel de Cervantes** (1547–1616) was the son of an impoverished aristocrat in Alcalá de Henares. Before making his home in Madrid, the author of *Don Quixote* learned the bitter truths of life in a Jesuit college, at the Battle of Lepanto where the Turks shattered his left arm, in Algerian captivity and in Spanish debtors' jails. The first part of *El ingenioso hidalgo don Quijote de la Mancha* was published in 1605 and proved an immediate success. In 1615, a plagiarized sequel forced Cervantes to complete the second part of his magnificent treatment of

Cervantes' hero Don Quixote and his companion Sancho Panza set forth in front of the monument to their creator.

idealistic dreams and cruel reality. Though his autobiographical short stories are almost equally masterful, Cervantes' poetry was unsuccessful and his numerous plays could never break through Lope de Vega's supremacy in the theatre.

Emblematic painter of Spain's often painful transition to a modern state, **Francisco de Goya** (1746–1828) began his Madrid career doing preparatory drawings for royal tapestries. He quickly graduated to

court portraits but, like Velázquez whose work he studied at the palace, painted his princes warts and all – even his beloved *Maja desnuda* has her faults. Made deaf, it is believed, by lead-poisoning, Goya became increasingly bitter in his treatment of aristocratic arrogance and social injustice. This culminated in his depicting the brutal violence of Madrid's struggle against the French in 1808 in the famous battle and execution scenes of *Dos de Mayo* and *Tres de Mayo*. He died in voluntary exile in Bordeaux.

Movida

Whether it has gone forever or is here to stay, the post-Franco creativity in Madrid expressed itself in the ephemeral culture of flashy, breathtaking advertising, photography, uninhibited comic strips, outlandish fashions and interior design.

In **music**, Madrid has been the most lively city on the national rock scene with singers such as **Luz Casal**, **Rosario** and the **Mecano** group. In jazz, **Pedro Iturralde** and **Jorge Pardo** are active, the latter working in the post-modern form of flamenco that with *nuevo flamenco* brings Andalucía to Madrid.

In the **cinema**, the acknowledged master has been **Pedro Almodóvar**, who has achieved international fame with *Women on the Edge of a Nervous Breakdown* and *Tie Me Up, Tie Me Down*. His studies of sexual excess, drugs and violence have epitomized the nervous reaction to the decades of national psychological repression and inhibition. It is perhaps a sign of the times that his latest films have been romantic comedies, calmer but still emotionally intense.

Goya, who was appointed First Royal Court Painter in 1799.

MUST SEE

A newcomer to Madrid may need help in choosing what to see in and around the city. Here are ten sights to include on any first visit, six in Madrid, and four from the surrounding region.

Museo del Prado★★★
(The Prado)
One of the world's leading museums, housing the splendid royal art collections of Velázquez, Goya, Titian, Hieronymus Bosch and Pieter Bruegel the Elder.

Museo Thyssen-Bornemisza★★★
(Thyssen-Bornemisza Museum)
One of Europe's great private art collections, ranging from Jan van Eyck through Caravaggio to 20C German Expressionists and Francis Bacon.

Palacio Real★★
(Royal Palace)
The imposing palace, built by the Bourbons, was the official royal residence until 1931. Explore the sumptuous apartments, the Throne Room and Banqueting Hall, and visit the Royal Armoury, Royal Carriage Museum and the lovely gardens.

Monasterio de las Descalzas Reales★★
(Descalzas Reales Convent)
This handsome, still-functioning convent of the barefoot *(descalzas)* nuns of St Clare is one of Madrid's few surviving Renaissance monuments. Its remarkable collection of religious art includes works by Titian and Rubens.

Plaza Mayor★★
A theatrical setting for the city's historic ceremonies at the heart of Habsburg Madrid, this elegant square is also a delightful place to take a morning coffee or an early evening drink.

Parque del Buen Retiro★★
(Retiro Park)
This large area of landscaped gardens not only provides refreshing respite from sightseeing, but also offers a range of recreational activities and entertainments, from folk-dancing and concerts to boating on the lake.

Toledo Catedral★★★
(Toledo Cathedral)
This grand edifice, begun in the 13C, has magnificent choir stalls and fine stained glass, and no fewer than 16 works by El Greco in the sacristy.

El Escorial★★★
(El Escorial Monastery and Palace)
Philip II's formidable
Renaissance palace and
monastery north-west of
Madrid, notable for its basilica,
royal apartments and pantheon
containing the remains of
Spanish monarchs.

Ávila's City Walls★★
Two kilometres (1 mile) of
beautifully preserved 11C city
walls are protected by 90 towers
and contain over 2 500 niches
for the medieval archers.

Segovia's Roman Aqueduct★★★
Built under Emperor Trajan
(1C), the majestic dry-stone
granite structure at Segovia is
over 700m (2 297ft) long and
was, until recently, still in
operation.

Toledo's imposing cathedral.

EXPLORING MADRID

THE CITY

The town was divided into neighbourhoods for Muslims, Jews and Christians, after Emir Mohammed I built his palace in 875, and ever since its citizens have referred to it in the plural, *los Madriles*. It is still true today. Architecturally, the city can be divided into distinct areas: Madrid de los Austrias (Habsburg Madrid), between Plaza Mayor and Puerta del Sol; Bourbon Madrid, separated from Habsburg Madrid by Paseo del Prado; and the modern city, north of Gran Vía. For the visitor, the town divides most simply into **Old Madrid**, **Modern**

The Royal Palace affords far-reaching views across Madrid.

Madrid and the **museums area** (principally the Golden Triangle consisting of the Prado, Thyssen-Bornemisza and Reina Sofía).

As churches and many shops close for the afternoon siesta while the main museums stay open all day, it is a good idea to do your street sightseeing early morning and late afternoon, and reserve your museum visits for midday. Large street maps posted outside each Metro station make it easy to find your way around. Following a time-honoured tradition, the names of many of the historic streets are displayed on attractive hand-painted ceramic tiles.

OLD MADRID

War, fire and over-ambitious city planning, particularly by Joseph Bonaparte and the Bourbons, have removed practically all trace of the Moorish city and many of the finer monuments of the Habsburg era. Yet a sense of the old city remains in the cluster of narrow streets south of **Calle Mayor**, where the Moors had their bazaar and the Christians of the Reconquista built their own shops, workshops, gaming-houses and brothels. Today, it is somewhat calmer and more respectable.

Puerta del Sol, one of the liveliest squares in Madrid.

Puerta del Sol

Historic in associations but thoroughly modern in atmosphere, the vast plaza lies at the very centre of the city. Indeed, a stone slab in the pavement outside the clocktower building of Madrid's regional government marks **Kilometre Zero**, the geographical centre of the country, from which all distances are measured. Sol (as the square is popularly known) takes its name 'Gate of the Sun' from a castle that was destroyed here during the insurrection of 15 cities against the monarchy in 1520.

The Oso y Madroño statue, a favourite meeting place.

At the corner of Calle del Carmen is the bronze **Oso y Madroño statue**, emblem of the city and, together with the fountain, a favourite meeting place. The oso is the bear and the madroño is a strawberry tree, symbolising forestry rights acquired in the 15C.

The **Metro station** opened up the country's first subway line in 1919, running north to Quatro Caminos. Bustling all day and most hours of the night, the plaza attracts shoppers to the major department store El Corte Inglés, the city's myriad gamblers to the jackpot machines and lottery kiosks, and New Year's Eve revellers to hear the midnight chiming of its clock tower. Following an age-old tradition, Spaniards swallow 12 grapes in time with the chimes.

Plaza Mayor★★

West of Puerta del Sol and just south of Calle
Mayor, the 'Main Square' was planned by
Philip II as the focus for his new capital's
royal ceremonies. It was finally laid out by
Juan Gómez de Mora for his son Philip III in
1619 and it is the latter's **equestrian statue**
that stands in the middle, the work of Italian
artists Giovanni da Bologna and Pietro Tacca.

Approached on all four sides through a
series of arched stairways, like passages into
an arena, the cobbled square is conceived in

*Take time for a
coffee and watch
the world go by in
the elegant Plaza
Mayor.*

the manner of an Italian piazza, a theatre with a spectacle to be watched by nobles on the balconies and by the common people in the shade of graceful arcades. The royal family watched from the much restored but decorative **Casa de la Panadería**, built between two slender bell-towers on the north side of the square and named after a bakery formerly located here. Of old, the spectacle might be a royal pageant, a bullfight on horseback, a gala première by Lope de Vega or an *auto da fe* confession and execution staged by the Inquisition. Today, the show is simply the world passing by: Madrileños and tourists sit at outdoor cafés and restaurants to chat and people-watch. On Sunday mornings stamp- and coin-collectors gather here, in summer, plays and concerts are staged, and in December there is a colourful Christmas market.

Plaza de la Villa★

Coin-collectors discuss an interesting find on the Sunday stalls.

Continue west along Calle Mayor to the peaceful square that groups three of the city's main architectural styles around a statue of Álvaro de Bazán, victor over the Turks at the naval battle of Lepanto in 1571. The 15C **Torre de los Lujanes** (Lujan Tower) on the east side of the square is one of the rare surviving examples of Mudéjar design, by Moorish architects working after the Reconquista. It is said to have held France's King François I for at least part of his 1525 imprisonment in Madrid. At the south end of the square is the 16C **Casa de Cisneros**, built for the nephew of the Inquisitor, Cardinal Cisneros. Its distinctively Spanish Renaissance style is known as Plateresque, from the Spanish *platero* meaning silversmith, featuring intricate

The Ayuntamiento (Town Hall) has impressive state apartments and a fine collection of tapestries.

detail reminiscent of a silversmith's craft. An arch links the house to the 17C **Ayuntamiento** (Town Hall), a fine baroque edifice originally designed by Gómez de Mora, architect of the Plaza Mayor. Its slate spires and towers are characteristic features of Habsburg Madrid. Behind it is the main city tourist office.

Iglesia de San Francisco el Grande

In a late-starting capital not noted for its churches, this 18C edifice makes a formidable impact, with its vast neo-classical façade and a colossal dome whose inner diameter measures 33m (108ft). Inside to

the left, the **Capilla de San Bernardino**
(Chapel of St Bernardino) has an early
painting by Goya (1781) over the altar. It
shows the saint preaching to the King of
Aragón and what is believed to be a self-
portrait of the artist (dressed in yellow,
second from the right). Note, too, the
Plateresque **choir stalls★**, brought here from
a monastery near Segovia.

Palacio Real★★ (Royal Palace)
Overlooking the Manzanares river, the
imposing mass of the sprawling edifice
closing off the west side of the city centre is a
clear expression of Spain's authoritarian
monarchy in the 18C. Today, the Spanish
royal family uses it only for formal
ceremonies, living in more modest

*San Francisco el
Grande contains
works by Goya,
Maella and Bayeu.*

The main entrance to the Royal Palace, facing the Plaza de la Armería.

Horseguards outside the Royal Palace.

apartments on the other side of town.

After the fire of 1734 destroyed the Habsburgs' Alcázar, shown in contemporary prints to be a charming hybrid of Moorish and Gothic, the Bourbon monarchs called on Italian and Spanish architects to design this neo-classical palace in the tradition of Louis XIV's Versailles. Built in white limestone and granite from the Guadarrama mountains, the long **façade** runs 140m (460ft), with alternating Ionic columns and Doric pilasters beneath a balustrade – the huge statues of the Spanish kings and queens originally intended to crown the palace have been installed on Plaza de

The monumental main staircase is decorated with fine frescoes by Corrado Giaquinto.

Oriente east of the palace and over in the Retiro Park.

Visits of the interior (entrance on Plaza de la Armería) are by guided tour only; including just 30 of the palace's 2 000 rooms, the tour is still something of a marathon. The imposing staircase leads through to the **Salón de Columnas** (Column Room). Among the highlights of the tour are the **Salón Gasparini**, a riot of rococo ornament, Alphonse XII's **Comedor de Gala** (Banqueting Hall) seating 145 guests, and above all the **Salón del Trono★** (Throne Room), with its décor of red velvet walls and gilded lions beneath the magnificent ceiling fresco of Spain's glories, painted by the Venetian master Tiepolo in 1764. Music lovers will appreciate the royal collection of Stradivarius instruments.

In an adjacent building, the **Real Armería★★** (Royal Armoury) is generally regarded as one of the finest collections of weapons and armour in the world. It displays the sword of 11C soldier-hero El Cid and the suit of armour of Charles V, plus the tools for bolting the parts together. The **Real Biblioteca** (Royal Library) includes a first edition of Cervantes' *Don Quixote* and the **Real Farmacia** (Royal Pharmacy) presents a set of elegant medicine cabinets to satisfy the most fastidious hypochondriac.

At the rear, the **Campo del Moro★** winter

Fountain in the palace winter gardens.

gardens, site of the 12C Moorish siege of the city after the Reconquista, provides an excellent view of the royal residence and the Manzanares Valley. The **Museo de Carruajes Reales★** (Royal Carriage Museum) here exhibits sumptuous royal vehicles from the 17C to the modern day.

Catedral de Nuestra Señora de la Almudena
(Cathedral of Our Lady of Almudena)
The gigantic but uninspiring cathedral south of the palace stands roughly on the site of the Moors' Great Mosque that was transformed into a church after the Christians captured the town in 1083. It was not until 1885 that the church hierarchy of

Nuestra Señora de la Almudena was rebuilt in neo-classical style after sustaining bomb damage during the Civil War.

Toledo grudgingly agreed to the Vatican granting Madrid the status of a diocese, with the accompanying right to a cathedral. In the spirit of its 19C conception, the church was originally neo-Gothic. It was bombed out in the Civil War and reconstructed with a neo-classical exterior in harmony with the royal palace, fulfilling the Spanish traditionalists' attachment to 'throne and altar'.
Inaugurated by Pope John Paul II in 1993, the church celebrates the city's founding legend of a statue of the Virgin Mary found in the city walls *(Almudena)* at the time of the Reconquista.

Plaza de Oriente

The square has had a hard time overcoming gloomy associations with the grim nationalistic speeches which Franco liked to give here, surrounded by oversize statues of the Christian Visigothic monarchs with whom he liked to identify. Neo-fascists still assemble here to observe the November anniversary of his death. But the place is brightened, especially on summer nights, by the terrace of the fashionable **Café de Oriente** and by the refurbished **Teatro Real** (Royal Theatre and Opera House), built in 1850. At the centre of the square is the heroic **equestrian statue of Philip IV**, a veritable *tour de force* by 17C baroque sculptor Pietro Tacca, a pupil of Giovanni da Bologna.

The plain exterior of the Descalzas Reales Convent belies the wealth of art treasures contained within.

Monasterio de las Descalzas Reales★★
(Descalzas Reales Convent)

At the corner of Plaza de San Martín, this retreat for aristocratic nuns is a true haven of tranquillity in a district of heavy traffic. The stricture of the royal ladies to go barefoot – *Descalzas Reales* – clearly does not entail any other vow of poverty. Founded in the 16C by Philip II's sister, Joanna of Austria, the convent of the sisters of St Clare is a rare and opulent Renaissance monument, richly endowed by noble patrons over the centuries and still functioning as a religious institution. The resident nuns working the vegetable gardens keep out of sight during visiting hours. Beyond the cloisters, an elaborately ornate staircase leads to the former **dormitories**, decorated by art treasures that include Zurbaran's fine portrait of St Francis and 17C Flemish tapestries designed by Rubens. The **Relicario** (Reliquary Chamber) assembles a quite astonishing collection of jewels and sacred relics, mostly bones of unidentified saints.

MODERN MADRID

Most of the modern city of interest to visitors is situated on the periphery of Habsburg Madrid, north of Gran Vía and east of Calle Toledo to Retiro Park. Its main attractions are the street life and *barrios* (neighbourhoods) rather than churches and monuments. All you need are good walking shoes and the time to stroll or sit around and watch the city's modern world go by.

Gran Vía

A dividing line between old and new Madrid, the city's main thoroughfare runs roughly west to east from Plaza de España, north of the Royal Palace, to join Calle de Alcalá at the great Plaza de la Cibeles. The non-stop traffic jam all day and much of the night is a spectacular display, with whistle-blowing police and car-honking drivers.

The busy modern city of Madrid, near Plaza de España.

Gran Vía was opened up in 1910 – through the demolition of 327 buildings and the suppression of 14 smaller streets – and its monumental banks, cinemas, hotels, nightclubs, department stores and offices embody the city's 20C flavour.

The architecture pays tribute, often in witty pastiches, to the Mudéjar, Gothic, Renaissance and baroque styles of the city's past. For admirers of commercial art, the cinemas' gigantic hand-painted **movie posters** are considered masterpieces of the genre. At the corner of Calle de Fuencarral, the stately **Telefónica Building** served as the Republicans' Civil War artillery position against the Nationalists occupying the Casa de Campo to the west.

Plaza de la Cibeles★

At the east end of Gran Vía, traffic swirls in perpetual paroxysm around the landmark 18C **fountain of Cybele**. The ancient fertility goddess, served by eunuch priests and extremely popular with Madrileños, is shown relaxing in a chariot drawn by a pair of watchful lions. But the plaza's most striking monument is the **Palacio de Comunicaciones**, the splendid yet stylistically indefinable post office, a secular cathedral completed in 1918 that visitor Leon Trotsky aptly nicknamed 'Our Lady of

Communications'. It is more fanciful than the reassuringly solid neo-classical **Banco de España** (Bank of Spain) across the plaza on the corner of **Calle de Alcalá**, Madrid's financial district.

The Paseos

Plaza de la Cibeles is also the junction of the broad, tree-lined boulevards, the Paseos, which provide the setting for that great Spanish institution, the *paseo* evening

The fountain of Cybele and Palacio de Comunicaciones are two of Madrid's great landmarks.

The busy junction of the Grand Vía and Calle de Alcalá at night.

promenade. Like the Italian *passeggiata*, it is the precious moment when the Madrid bourgeoisie and young couples take a stroll, to see and be seen, to talk of politics and bullfights, love and football. The Paseos have also witnessed the triumphal processions of Habsburg and Bourbon monarchs, of Franco's victorious army in 1939 and a million defiant Madrileños demonstrating for democracy in 1981. To the south, underlining the explicitly social function, the **Paseo del Prado★** was also known as the *Salón*. Its prestige is emphasized by two veritable monuments of luxury, the Ritz and Palace hotels facing each other across the grand **Neptune Fountain** on Plaza Cánovas del Castillo. To the north, **Paseo de Recoletos** extends into **Paseo de la Castellana**, with fashionable *terrazas* (terrace cafés and restaurants) along the grass strip in the middle.

Parque del Buen Retiro** (Retiro Park)

Within easy reach of the Prado and the other main museums, this delightful park offers a good opportunity to get away from the bustle of the traffic and the hard slog of sightseeing.

It originally provided a good retreat – hence its name – for Philip II while he was waiting for El Escorial to be completed. Its grounds belonged to the 15C monastery of San Jerónimo and to a later palace of Philip IV, both now destroyed.

There are numerous attractions scattered across its 130 hectares (321 acres) of French-style formal and English-style landscaped gardens: folk-dancing, concerts, a June book

The delightful Retiro Park offers a refreshing retreat from the noise of the city.

A captive audience for the puppet show in Retiro Park.

fair; art exhibitions in the **Palacio de Cristal** and **Palacio de Velázquez**; summer film shows at **La Chopera**; boats for hire on the oblong pond of **El Estanque**; and weekend **puppet shows** in the north-west corner, near the Puerta de Alcalá entrance.

Cortes

West of the Paseo del Prado, between Calle de Alcalá and Calle Huertas, is the largely 19C district around the **Cortes Españolas** (Spanish Parliament). Visitors are admitted on Saturday mornings to the rather undistinguished building of the lower house (Congress), and are shown the chamber with the bullet holes left by Colonel Antonio Tejero in his abortive coup of 1981 (*see* p.17).

Just to the north, on Calle de Alcalá, the

Círculo de Bellas Artes (Fine Arts Circle) is a highly agreeable cultural centre offering one-day membership access to its art galleries, concert hall, theatre, cinema and a bar in handsome, comfortable surroundings.

South of the Cortes, on Calle de Cervantes, the **Casa de Lope de Vega** (home of the playwright) includes an attractive reconstruction of the great writer's 17C Madrid. By ironic coincidence – for they hated each other – **Cervantes' burial place** is on Calle Lope de Vega, in the Trinitaria Convent, but this is rarely open to visitors.

A little further to the south is the lively **Calle Huertas** bar district. Here, the bars are more genteel than the *Movida*-style ones of the Malasaña district, and are highly recommended – as are the restaurants and

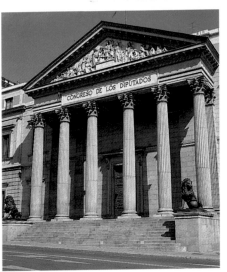

The neo-classical entrance to the Spanish Parliament is flanked by a pair of bronze lions cast from cannons captured in the Moroccan War (1860).

ope de Vega's ouse has been reserved as a museum.

bars further west, on and around the delightful **Plaza de Santa Ana**.

Malasaña

Situated between the Gran Vía and Calle de Sagasta is the Malasaña district. This *barrio* (quarter) is beloved of Madrileños as the home of the Malasaña family, martyred on 2 May 1808 in the insurrection against Napoleonic troops that is commemorated annually on **Plaza del Dos de Mayo**.

The plaza's bouncy *terraza* cafés and music bars have prospered since the progressive spirit of the quarter was revived in the post-Franco era. When Malasaña became the major focus of the *Movida*, the poster advertising the *Dos de Mayo* celebrations showed Goya's hero with his arms raised before the firing squad – and an electronic guitar around his waist.

Chueca

Like Malasaña, the adjacent *barrio* of Chueca, west of the Paseo de Recoletos, remains one of the liveliest neighbourhoods of modern Madrid and is the hub of the city's gay scene. On and around **Calle Almirante** are several attractive art galleries, fashionable boutiques and restaurants. At night, the more cautious may prefer to avoid the area immediately around **Plaza de Chueca** itself, which is notorious for drug-dealers.

In the neighbourhood's north-west corner, a decorative note of respectability is added by the ornate Churrigueresque baroque façade of the **Museo Municipal** (Municipal Museum) on Calle Fuencarral. Maps and models of old Madrid trace the rapid growth of the city.

El Rastro

South of Plaza Mayor, Madrid's monumental
flea-market sprawls along and around
Ribera de Curtidores down to the Ronda de
Toledo. It operates principally at the
weekends, but antiques dealers and junk
shops are open on week days – the best time
to come if you want to browse and haggle in
quiet. But the rollicking folklore, especially
on Sunday mornings, is not to be missed. As
with all big-city flea-markets, visitors need to
be wary of fakes and pick-pockets.

*Looking for a
bargain at the El
Rastro flea-market.*

Puerta de Toledo

Puerta de Toledo, one of Madrid's two surviving city gates, was completed in 1817.

This triumphal arch was originally built to welcome Napoleon Bonaparte in the Peninsular War, but he never made it. It now provides an imposing backdrop to the **Mercado Puerta Toledo**, transformed from the municipal fish market into a high-class and attractive shopping centre for (genuine) designer clothes and antiques.

THE MUSEUMS

For many visitors the greatest treasures of
Madrid are its museums. Take them in
manageable doses. The so-called 'Golden
Triangle' along the Paseo del Prado,
between Plaza Cánovas del Castillo and
Atocha railway station, groups the Prado,
Thyssen-Bornemisza and the Reina Sofía.
The Prado needs at least a day to explore
comfortably, but the other two could be
visited in the same day.

To help you avoid the temptation of trying
to cram too much in, the modern
collections of the Reina Sofía are open on
Mondays when the other two are closed.
There are also a couple of other noteworthy
museums for those with the time and
inclination.

Museo del Prado*** (The Prado)
The royal collections assembled here are so
rich in quality and variety that to do them
justice needs some planning – and for

*The Prado Museum
houses the royal
family's collections
of art, providing an
outstanding
overview of Spanish
art.*

newcomers, some self-discipline in concentrating on the paintings they really want to see most.

Originally built in 1785 as a natural science museum, the Prado was established in 1819 by Ferdinand VII as the Royal Museum of Painting and Sculpture to house the huge collections of the Habsburg and Bourbon monarchs, much expanded since then by donations and acquisitions. Today, only one-tenth of the thousands of works are on display at any one time.

Ongoing renovation and reorganization of the collections may change some of the arrangement of the works exhibited. At present, since the main entrance on the Paseo del Prado, **Puerta de Velázquez**, is usually used by large groups, individuals are advised to use the side entrances, **Puerta de Goya** on Calle Felipe IV or **Puerta de Murillo** on Plaza de Murillo. The **main floor** (*planta principal*, above the street level) is devoted to the Spanish masters from the 16C to the 18C (El Greco, Velázquez,

One of the Prado's galleries.

Zurbarán, Murillo and Goya) and the
Italians (Fra Angelico, Mantegna, Botticelli,
Titian and Veronese). The street-level **lower
floor** (*planta baja*) exhibits the northern
European Flemish, Dutch and German
schools (Bosch, Bruegel, Rubens, Dürer and
Rembrandt) and Spanish art from the 12C
to the 16C, plus Goya's so-called *Black*

El Greco's The
Adoration of the
Shepherds.

Paintings. The annex in the nearby 17C **Casón del Buen Retiro★**, a relic of the old palace of Philip IV, houses Spanish paintings of the 19C and 20C.

We propose here a selection of the museum's most important painters and their masterpieces.

Spanish★★★

El Greco (1541–1614) Signed Domenikos Theotokopoulos, *Nobleman with his Hand on his Chest* is an early work of realism from shortly after the Cretan-born painter arrived in Toledo, epitomizing the Spanish aristocrat in austere but elegant costume and serene yet unbendingly serious demeanour. Executed at the end of his life,

Velázquez's vast work The Surrender of Breda *records the defeated Dutch general Nassau before the Spanish commander Espínola.*

The Adoration of the Shepherds projects the artist's fervent spirituality, with dematerialized, almost surreal, human figures.

Diego Velázquez (1599–1660) The Prado's most celebrated picture, the endlessly hypnotic *Maids of Honour* (*Las Meninas*) presents the artist himself coolly appraising his royal masters, their servants – and us – with stunning command of space and colour. He tackles with equal facility and breathtaking technique a formal military scene such as *The Surrender of Breda*, a piercing psychological portraiture of *Philip IV*, and subjects of the common people, such as *The Drunkards*.

José Ribera (1591–1661) More Italian than Spanish after a long career in Naples, he uses in *Archimedes* a cheerful Neapolitan as a model for the august Greek scholar. The debt to Caravaggio's strongly contrasting light and shade is also evident in the dramatic *Martyrdom of St Philip*.

Francisco de Zurbarán (1598–1664) The graceful portrait of a defiant Spanish lady as *Santa Casilda* and the *Tavern* still-life of carafes and a goblet are outstanding examples of the naturalist style of this mystic who is best known for his scenes of monastic life.

Bartolomé Murillo (1618–1682) The sentimental but often highly personal charm of Murillo's religious pictures are exemplified in the portrayal of Jesus as a pretty little boy in *Good Shepherd* and a soulful Mary in the *The Escorial Immaculate Conception*.

Francisco de Goya (1746–1828) A revolutionary spirit is omnipresent. In *Wine Harvest*, aristocrats enjoy their grapes, oblivious of the hard-working labourers

Goya's celebrated portrayal of Charles IV and his family (1800).

behind them. The unflattering *The Family of Charles IV* shows the king's wife, Maria Luisa, very much in charge. The emblematic *Dos de Mayo* and *Tres de Mayo* depict the violence of Madrid's heroic fight against the French in 1808. Even the seductive *Clothed Maya* and *Naked Maya* express an impudence in the strangely superimposed heads.

Italian★★
Renaissance masters include **Fra Angelico** (an exquisite *Annunciation*); **Botticelli** (*Nastagio degli Onesti*, three panels illustrating a story from Boccaccio's *Decameron*); **Antonello da Messina** (a tragic *Dead Christ Supported by an Angel*); **Andrea**

EXPLORING MADRID

Mantegna (*Death of the Virgin*); **Raphael** (a mysterious portrait, *The Cardinal*, and the superb *Christ Falling on the Way to Calvary*).

Venetian masters include **Titian** (an exemplary equestrian portrait of his patron, *Emperor Charles V*, and the bawdy *Bacchanal*); **Tintoretto** (the theatrical panorama of *Christ Washing the Disciples' Feet*); **Veronese** (an unusually playful *Venus and Adonis*); and the museum's one great **Caravaggio**, *David and Goliath*, which was so influential on Spanish painting of the Golden Age.

Flemish*** and Dutch
Rogier van der Weyden (the *Descent from the Cross* altarpiece, widely considered his finest picture); **Hans Memling** (a delicate *Birth of Christ* triptych); **Hieronymus Bosch** (three absolute masterpieces of surrealist eroticism and apocalypse, four centuries before the modern movement: *Garden of Delights*, *Table of the Seven Deadly Sins* and *The Hay Cart*); **Pieter Bruegel the Elder** (the profoundly humanistic and poignant *Triumph of Death*); **Rubens** (*Three Graces*, characteristically buxom, and an opulent *Adoration of the Magi*); and the museum's one authentic **Rembrandt**, *Queen Artemisia*, symbol of marital fidelity, painted at the time of the master's own marriage.

German
Albrecht Dürer (the penetrating *Self-Portrait* and a graceful duo, *Adam* and *Eve*); **Hans Baldung Grien** (*Ages of Man and Death*).

Museo Thyssen-Bornemisza***
(Thyssen-Bornemisza Museum)
At Paseo del Prado 8, the neo-classical Palacio de Villahermosa houses one of the

The magnificently restored Palacio de Villahermosa now houses the Thyssen-Bornemisza Museum.

world's greatest private art collections, inaugurated in 1993. Some 800 works, from the 14C to the present day, were donated by German-born industrialist Baron Hans Thyssen at the prompting of his Spanish wife, Tita Cervera. (The former 'Miss Spain' is portrayed in the foyer with the baron, King Juan Carlos and his queen.) The baron's father, Heinrich, assembled the bulk of the collection in the 1920s, advised by the greatest art historians of the day.

The works are organized chronologically on three floors, from the top down, with a bar and cafeteria in the basement.

Second Floor: European (14C–18C)

Italian primitives (Duccio di Buoninsegna); Early Flemish (Jan van Eyck, Rogier van der Weyden and Petrus Christus); Renaissance portraits (Ghirlandaio, Hans Memling, Hans Holbein, Carpaccio and Titian); German masters (Dürer, Lucas Cranach and Hans

Baldung Grien); Spanish (El Greco and
Zurbarán); Caravaggio, his disciple Ribera,
and a rare Bernini sculpture.

First Floor: European and American (17C–20C)

Dutch (Frans Hals); American (Whistler,
Winslow Homer); English (Gainsborough,
Constable); Impressionists and Post-
Impressionists (Monet, Manet, Degas,
Gauguin, Van Gogh, Toulouse-Lautrec,
Cézanne); Expressionists (Edvard Munch,
Egon Schiele, George Grosz, Ernst Ludwig
Kirchner and Max Beckmann).

Ground Floor: 20C

European (Picasso, Braque, Juan Gris,
Mondrian, Kandinsky, Magritte, Francis
Bacon, Lucien Freud); American (Edward
Hopper, Jackson Pollock, Mark Rothko,
Robert Rauschenberg).

Picasso's Guernica *(1937) is the centrepiece of the Reina Sofía collection.*

Museo Nacional Centro de Arte Reina Sofía★ (Queen Sofia Art Centre)

At the south end of Paseo del Prado facing Atocha station, the handsome modern transformation of a sprawling 18C hospital completes the city's Golden Triangle, with a fine collection of 20C Spanish art. Its centrepiece is Picasso's **Guernica★★★**. This monumental denunciation of the German bombing of the Basque city in the Spanish Civil War took a long time getting here. Picasso first hung it in the Spanish Republican pavilion at the Paris Exposition of 1937, and then sent it to New York's Museum of Modern Art, where it was to stay until, as he said, democracy returned to Spain. It was transferred to Madrid in 1981, at first in a much criticized display at the Casón del Buen Retiro before finally moving to the Reina Sofía in 1992. Here the stark work in black, grey and white is beautifully

Works by modern painters are exhibited on the second floor in the Reina Sofía.

exhibited, surrounded by preparatory studies and what the artist calls 'post-scripts' – moving detailed treatments of a mourning mother, a screaming horse and other symbolic elements of Guernica's suffering. Besides Picasso's earlier work, the museum also exhibits Salvador Dalí, Juan Gris, Joan Miró, Tàpies and Chillida.

Museo Arqueológico Nacional★★
(National Archaeological Museum)
Sharing the premises of the **Biblioteca Nacional** (National Library), Calle de Serrano 13, the collection traces Spain's origins, from the Stone Age through Roman times to medieval Christian and Islamic art. Among the more noteworthy pieces are two ornately carved **Celto-Iberian statues** (4C BC), the aristocratic **Lady of Elche★★★** and a goddess, **Lady of Baza★★**, plus a hoard of 8C **Visigothic jewels★★** recently unearthed in Toledo.

Museo Lázaro Galdiano★★
Housed in the neo-classical palace of the donor (Calle de Serrano 122), this personal collection is remarkable above all for its Spanish art, including El Greco, Murillo, Zurbarán, Ribera and some of

The National Library, built in 1892, has an ornate granite façade. It was one of the first constructions in Spain to be built with an iron framework.

Goya's more disturbing *Black Paintings*.
There are also important Flemish works by
Bosch and Quentin Matsys and an exquisite
collection of jewels, ivories, precious
enamels★★ and antique clocks.

OTHER ATTRACTIONS

Casa de Campo★ behind the Royal Palace
An ideal spot for a day in the country
without leaving town, where you can walk,
picnic, swim (in pools), go boating or visit
the amusement park and zoo. The parkland
was reafforested by Philip II in 1559.
Cine Doré Santa Isabel 3 [Map:LZ]
The city's oldest cinema (1922), now home
of the Filmoteca Nacional (National
Cinematheque), with an Art Nouveau
façade.
Real Monasterio de la Encarnación★
(Royal Convent of the Incarnation) square of
the same name [Map:KX]
Augustine convent founded by Marguerite
of Austria, wife of Philip III; 17C paintings,
and an astonishing **Relicario★** (Relics
Room).
Faro de la Moncloa (Moncloa Beacon)
north of Parque del Oeste
An observation tower erected in 1992; it is
76m (250ft) high with a fine view from the
balcony★★ over the city and the Meseta
plateau.
Jardín Botánico (Botanical Garden)
south of the Prado [Map:NZ]
Cool shady gardens opened to the public in
1781 and renovated in the 1980s.
Jardines de las Vistillas (Gardens with Vistas)
south of the cathedral [Map:KYZ]
Terrace cafés with **views★** across the
Manzanares river to Sierra de Guadarrama.

*The Art Nouveau
Cine Doré.*

La Corrala In colourful Lavapiés quarter, Calle Sombrerete [Map:LZ]
This balconied tenement building was declared a national monument for its cultural activities.

Museo Cerralbo★ Calle Ventura Rodríguez 17 [Map:KV]
Marqués de Cerralbo's grand mansion has been transformed into a museum of 19C aristocratic life, displaying paintings, furniture and porcelain, armour and weaponry.

Museo de América★ (Museum of the Americas) Ciudad Universitaria, Avenida Reyes Católicos 6
Artefacts from Latin America, including pre-Columbian art, the **Cortesano Manuscript★★★** (one of only four Mayan manuscripts) and the **Treasure of Los Quimbayas★**.

The delightful shaded Botanical Garden, where you can relax and unwind away from the bustle of the city.

64

The Plaza de España, where old and modern Madrid meet, is a popular promenade for Madrileños.

Museo Nacional de Artes Decorativas
(Decorative Arts Museum) Calle de Montalbán, 12 [Map:NX]
Fine Spanish glass, ceramics, porcelain and jewellery.

Museo del Ejército★ (Army Museum)
Calle Méndez Núñez 1 [Map:NY]
Covers military history from ancient times to the Civil War; includes El Cid's sword and *Conquistadores* armour.

Museo Naval (Maritime Museum)
Paseo del Prado 5 [Map:NXY – M³]
A collection of **model ships★**, navigational instruments and charts, dating back to the first Spanish voyages to the Americas and including the **map★★** of Juan de la Cosa, the earliest known map of America.

Museo Romántico Calle de San Mateo 13 [Map:LV]
Costumes, jewellery and furniture, dating

from the crinolined age of rococo.

Palacio de Liria Calle de la Princesa 20 [Map:KV]
The splendid residence of the Duchess of
Alba; the private picture gallery is open only
by appointment.

Palacio de Santa Cruz Plaza Provincia 1, east
of Plaza Mayor [Map:LY]
Former court prison, whose inmates
included Lope de Vega. Now houses the
Ministry for Foreign Affairs.

Parque del Oeste★ (West Park) north of the
Royal Palace
This refreshing parkland includes the
ancient Egyptian Temple of Debod (4C BC),
salvaged from the Nile Valley, when the
Aswan Dam was built.

Plaza de Colón (Columbus Square) [Map:NV]
Christopher Columbus's statue stands above
a subterranean cultural centre, with films,
theatre and exhibitions.

Plaza de España [Map:KV]
Skyscrapers surround Cervantes' monument

*The statue of
Columbus, on the
Plaza de Colón.*

*San Fernando Roya
Fine Arts Academy.*

of Don Quixote on horseback, with Sancho Panza on his donkey.

Plaza de la Paja [Map:KZ]

The acacia trees and fountain make this one of the old city's most charming squares, a refuge of quiet shade in summer.

Plaza Monumental de las Ventas★ (Bullring) Calle Alcalá, east of Salamanca quarter

Considered by *aficionados* to be the high temple of bullfighting arenas, this is the biggest in Spain, seating 22 300 spectators.

Puerta de Alcalá★ (Alcalá Arch) Plaza de la Independencia [Map:NX]

A triumphal arch built in the 18C to welcome Charles III to Madrid.

This striking statue announces the great bullfighting arena of Madrid.

The church of San Isidro stands in the heart of the old town, close to the Plaza Mayor.

Real Academia de Bellas Artes de San Fernando★ (San Fernando Royal Fine Arts Academy) Calle de Alcalá [Map:LX – M²]
Contains a fine collection of works, by Velázquez, Zurbarán, Goya and Rubens, among others.
Real Fábrica de Tapices (Royal Tapestry Factory) Calle de Fuenterrabía 8. Near Atocha station
The factory, founded in 1721 by Philip V, is still using Goya's designs for tapestries.
San Antonio de la Florida near Norte station
An 18C chapel with Goya **frescoes★★** and the artist's tomb.
Iglesia de San Ginés Calle del Arenal 13 [Map:KY]

This church, dating back to Moorish rule, contains El Greco's painting, *Money Changers Chased from Temple*.

Iglesia de San Isidro Calle de Toledo 49 [Map:KZ]

The massive domed church of the city's patron saint, San Isidro, was the town's cathedral until Nuestra Señora de la Almudena was completed.

San Jerónimo el Real near Casón del Buen Retiro [Map:NY]

Juan Carlos was crowned in the abbey church of the long-gone monastery.

Pontificia de San Miguel Calle San Justo 4, south-west of Plaza Mayor [Map:KY]

An 18C Italian baroque basilica, with an attractively curving façade.

San Miguel church has an imposing curved granite façade.

Iglesia de San Pedro south of Plaza de la Villa [Map:KY]

A 14C church, with a rare Mudéjar tower.

Santiago Bernabeu Stadium Del Padre Damián, off La Castellana

The city's most sacred secular shrine – the football stadium of Real Madrid and the Spanish national team.

El Pardo 9km (5 miles) north-west of Madrid

This town originated round a royal palace, Franco's former residence, and is now popular for its open-air *terraza* restaurants.

EXCURSIONS FROM MADRID

All the excursions we propose here can be made comfortably in a day. However, some people may like to plan an overnight stay in Toledo for a more leisurely visit. Segovia or Ávila can be combined in a single round trip with an overnight stay in one of those towns.

TOLEDO★★★

All the strands of Spanish history and culture come together in this magnificent,

Majestic Toledo sits on a granite hill overlooking the Tagus river and the Meseta plains.

luminous hilltop town 70km (44 miles) south of Madrid. Dominating a loop in the Tagus river, the magical skyline of the Gothic cathedral flanked by the Alcázar fortress and San Juan monastery is a constant background in the paintings of El Greco, who made Toledo his home town. Its elevated position in the southern Meseta plain prompted the Romans to create the strategic garrison town of Toletum, which the Visigoths in turn made their capital in the 6C.

In the Middle Ages, Jews, Christians and Muslims enriched its cultural life, their sages working together to transmit the knowledge of Hebrew, Greek and Arabic scholarship. This enlightenment came to an end in the growing intolerance of the Reconquista, but Toledo retained its pre-eminence in the Spanish church even after the political capital was transferred to Madrid.

For a first truly awe-inspiring **view★★★** of the town, take the Puente de Alcántara (Alcántara Bridge) over the river to the numerous observation terraces on the Carretera de Circunvalación road running around the southern periphery. Once inside the town, lose yourself happily in the narrow winding streets that are the most obvious legacy of its cosmopolitan past and come across both its great monuments and other lesser, unsung beauties by serendipity – and an occasional signpost.

Catedral★★★ (Cathedral)

The silhouette of the great 13C church, more French Gothic than Spanish, can be appreciated only at a distance as its bulk is swallowed up in the maze of tiny streets around it. It took over 250 years to complete and, like the imposing tower, the three portals of the main façade on Plaza del Ayuntamiento, most notably the profusely sculpted central **Puerta del Perdón** (Gate of Pardon), date from the 15C.

Enter left of this façade through the Puerta del Mollete past the cloister to the north side of the church. In the centre of the five-aisled interior, behind a fine Renaissance grill, is the **choir** with magnificently carved **stalls★★★**. The 16C wood panels recount in dramatic detail the conquest of Grenada, while the upper levels in alabaster portray scenes of the Old

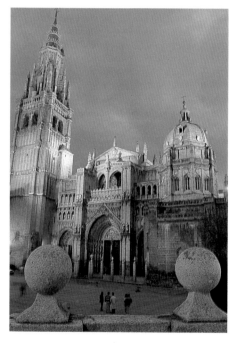

The magnificent cathedral, one of Spain's finest Gothic buildings, provides splendid views from its north tower.

Testament. In the **Capilla Mayor** (Main Chapel) east of the Choir, the monumental **retable**★★ recounts the life of Jesus in five tiers of polychrome sculpture. In the ambulatory behind the chapel, the lavish 18C baroque **Transparente**, ornate screens in marble, jasper and bronze which are illuminated by an opening cut in the ceiling.

The **Sala Capitular** (Chapter House) has a handsome **Mudéjar ceiling**★. 'Mudéjar' refers to the highly decorative architectural style developed by Muslims converted after the Reconquista. Among the cardinals' portraits are two by Goya. The **Sacristy** contains 16 **paintings**★ by El Greco, works by Titian, Van Dyck and Goya, and ceiling frescoes by Luca Giordano.

Iglesia de Santo Tomé

With its fine medieval Mudéjar tower, this church is visited for the city's most famous wall painting, El Greco's **Burial of the Count of Orgaz** ★★★(1586). In masterful juxtaposition of the mystical and realistic, it recounts the miraculous participation of St Augustine and St Stephen in the 14C count's funeral. Among the celestial spectators is Philip II, still alive at the time of the painting.

Casa y Museo de El Greco★
(El Greco House and Museum)

Down the hill from the church, the house said to have been the painter's home is in what was the old Jewish quarter (Judería). The house was originally built by 14C financier Samuel Ha-Levi, financial adviser to Peter I of Castile (until the king lived up to his nickname of Peter the Cruel by killing him and confiscating his fortune). It has been restored in vague approximation of

El Greco's 16C studio. More interesting is the adjacent museum with some works of the master, including a view of the city.

Synagogues

Only two of the ten synagogues in the Jewish quarter still exist today. The **Sinagoga del Tránsito★★** (Synagogue of the Dormition) was built in 1355 by Samuel Ha-Levi. It was transformed into a church after the expulsion of the Jews, hence the name and the vestiges of Christian tombs. In the simple rectangular interior, with an upper gallery for women worshippers, Muslim artists crafted the stucco work in fine Mudéjar style, with intricate filigree decoration and inscriptions in Hebrew and Arabic praising God, the king and Ha-Levi. The adjacent **Museo Sefardí** (Sephardic Museum) traces the history of Toledo's Jewish community from Roman times until its expulsion in 1492.

Originally the most important Jewish house of worship in Toledo, the Muslim-built **Sinagoga de Santa María la Blanca★** (St Mary the White) became a church after the Expulsion. With its horseshoe arches on 24 octagonal pillars, it still resembles a mosque.

Alcázar

There have been fortresses on this site since the days of the Roman *castrum*, but they have been repeatedly destroyed in war, most recently in the Spanish Civil War in 1936. With the rest of the city in Republican hands, the Alcázar was occupied by pro-Franco forces and their families during a devastating 72-day siege. In a famous response to a telephone call warning him his

son would be executed if the Nationalists did not surrender, their commander, Colonel José Moscardó, told his boy: 'Pray to God, shout "Viva España" and die like a hero.' (A month later, the son was shot, but in reprisal for an air raid.) Franco finally sent in more Nationalist troops to relieve the beleaguered forces – and restored the Alcázar as a monument of fascist heroism. Roughly as originally designed for Emperor Charles V, it is still in part occupied by the army.

Near by, the triangular **Plaza de Zocodover** stands on the site of the Moorish

The 16C Alcázar stands at Toledo's highest point, on the site of a Roman fort.

market. The Inquisition staged its executions here. It is now a popular meeting place for Toledans on their evening *paseo*.

Museo de Santa Cruz★★
(Santa Cruz Museum)

With its elegant arcaded patio, the attractive 16C Renaissance building, built as a hospital, has been transformed into a museum. In addition to works by Ribera and Goya, there are 18 **paintings★** by El Greco, including the **Altarpiece of the Assumption★**, a late work of remarkable intensity.

Details from the façade of Santa Cruz Museum.

Other Attractions

Cristo de la Luz (Christ of the Light)
An early 11C nine-domed mosque, transformed into a church but still used for worship by visiting Muslims.

Hospital de Tavera★ (Tavera Hospital)
This 16C hospital, built outside the city walls, has important works by Tintoretto, Ribera and El Greco, including the latter's last work, **Baptism of Christ★★**.

Puerta del Sol
The 14C 'Gate of the Sun' is a fine example of Mudéjar design, featuring two horseshoe arches.

Monasterio de San Juan de los Reyes★
(St John of the Kings Monastery)
A 15C monastery built by Ferdinand and Isabella in a mixture of Gothic, Renaissance and Mudéjar styles.

Iglesia de San Román
Mudéjar church with 13C frescoes of the Councils of Toledo and now a museum devoted to Visigothic culture.

EL ESCORIAL★★★
(El Escorial Monastery and Palace)
Some 45km (28 miles) north-west of Madrid, Philip II's palace and adjoining San Lorenzo monastery express perfectly the essence of the sombre, single-minded creator of Spain's modern capital. In a resolutely Spanish interpretation of Italian Renaissance design, architect Juan de Herrera completed in 1584 a massive monument to his master's piety and authoritarian monarchy.

The rectangle of grey granite, 206m (676ft) long and 161m (528ft) wide, encloses royal apartments, a church, a mausoleum, a monastery and a museum. It is gigantic, with 86 stairways, 1 200 doors and 2 600 windows. The king had it all laid out in a grid-plan to symbolize the martyrdom of San Lorenzo, the Spanish-born saint roasted alive on a grill in Rome in AD 258 – the grill is the Escorial's omnipresent emblem. (It was on the saint's day, 10 August 1557, after defeating the French in battle, that Philip II had decided to build El Escorial.)

*he austere yet
majestic design of
l Escorial
Monastery was a
eaction to the
xcessively ornate
rchitectural styles
f Charles V's reign.*

For a fine overall **view★** of the walled compound, drivers can follow signs 7km (4 miles) west from the town of San Lorenzo de El Escorial to **Silla de Felipe II** (Seat of Philip II), a group of boulders on a rise overlooking the site, where the king is said to have come to survey construction progress.

Palacios★★ (Royal Apartments)

On the second floor, built deliberately around the apse of the church, the **Habitaciones de Felipe II** (Philip II's Apartments) are austere in the extreme. The rooms are small and, apart from the 16C Flemish tapestries in the **Salón del Trono** (Throne Room), the furnishings are modest. A door in the king's bedroom opens to the church so that, when he lay dying in 1598 at the age of 71, he could participate in Mass from his bed. Still there is the chair on which he rested his gouty leg and, in another room, the sedan in which he had to be carried about. Away from the church in the north-east corner, the third-floor **Palacio de los Borbones** (Bourbon Apartments), renovated in the 18C, are more spacious, with ornate inlaid panelling and lively **tapestries★** based on designs by Rubens and, most notably, Goya's scenes of popular festivities.

In the handsome **Biblioteca★★** (Library), Herrera designed the shelves for Philip II's great collection of Arabic manuscripts and rare books, including St Theresa of Ávila's diary of her ecstatic dreams. Two new **museums★★** house Spanish, Flemish and Italian masters (**Museo de Pintura**, Picture Museum) and an architectural display devoted to the Escorial's original construction (**Museo de Arquitectura**, Architectural Museum).

Basilica** and Monastery

The church's interior follows the Greek-cross plan of St Peter's, Rome, its huge cupola soaring 92m (302ft) above the transept crossing, supported by four giant pillars. The 17C **ceiling frescoes** are the work of Luca Giordano. Herrera's monumental high altar, with columns of red marble, onyx and jasper, has bronze statues by Leoni and Pompeo Leoni. Father and son, they also carved the statuary for the **mausoleums** of Charles V and Philip II on either side of the choir. In a chapel to the left is a superb white marble Crucifixion by **Benvenuto Cellini** (1562).

Much of the royal art collection here has been progressively moved to the Prado, but the **Sacristía** (Sacristy) and **Salas Capitulares** (Chapter Houses) have several fine paintings of Velázquez, El Greco, Ribera, Veronese, Tintoretto and Titian and two works by Hieronymus Bosch, including a second version of *The Haywain*.

The **Panteón de los Reyes**★★★ (Royal Pantheon) is a 17C octagonal chapel beneath the church choir. Here, stacked in tiers of four, are the gilded marble tombs of all but three of Spain's monarchs since Charles V, kings to the left and child-bearing queens to the right. (Missing are the first two Bourbons: Philip V who is buried in the Palacio de la Granja, and Ferdinand VI who was laid to rest in Madrid.) In the 19C **Panteón de los Infantes**★ (Children's Pantheon) are the tombs of some 30 royal infants – and the childless queens.

SEGOVIA★★★

This proud city enjoys a picturesque **setting**★★ perched on a triangular rock north of the Sierra de Guadarrama. In its 15C heyday, its favour with the kings and queens of Castilla meant that for a while it might have succeeded Toledo as capital of Spain rather than the less prestigious Madrid.

It is a handsome town in which some of the remaining fortifications serve as sustaining walls for dwellings, with many of the older quarters built in the region's attractive honey-coloured stone. It has also preserved several characteristic Castilian

The hilltop position of Segovia provides magnificent views across the Sierra de Guadarrama, especially from the towers of the Alcázar.

Romanesque churches with Mudéjar minaret-
like towers, all much older than the cathedral.

Acueducto Romano★★★
(Roman Aqueduct)
Built in all likelihood under Emperor Trajan
in the 1C, this masterpiece of elegant
Roman engineering on the south side of
town brought in water from the Acebeda
river, well into the 20C. The two-tiered
structure, built of local granite without
mortar, is 728m (2 388ft) long and reaches
28m (92ft) in height where the ground is at
its lowest, over the Plaza del Azoguejo.

Alcázar★
Soaring over the confluence of the Eresma
and Clamores rivers are the pepperpot
towers, dungeon and fanciful battlements of
the royal castle. In fact the Alcázar itself is a
pastiche: after being ravaged by fire in 1862,
the fortress was reconstucted in a romantic

*Perched on a cliff
overlooking the
valley, Segovia's
Alcázar resembles
fairytale castle.*

*A testament to the
engineering skills of
the Romans, the
aqueduct at Segovia
was in use until
recently, bringing
water to the city
from the Acebeda
river.*

pseudo-medieval style. The Alcázar served as the setting for the marriage of Philip II to Anne of Austria in 1570. In more recent times, the keep was used to incarcerate political prisoners. Visitors who climb the 152 stairs to the summit of the dungeon will be rewarded with a great **view** over the city and the Sierra de Guadarrama.

Catedral★★ (Cathedral)

The last of Spain's major Gothic churches was begun in 1525 under Charles V after the original was destroyed in the Comuneros' Revolt in 1511. In contrast to the Flamboyant Gothic exterior, the interior is surprisingly austere, almost completely devoid of sculpture and other decoration. The 15C **choir stalls** were salvaged from the old cathedral. Its **cloisters**, too, were transported here, piece by piece. Notice

The impressive Gothic cathedral dominates the Castilian city of Segovia.

the fine 17C Flemish tapestries in the chapter house.

Plaza de San Martín★

In the middle of a pleasant shopping area, this medieval plaza is in fact two squares on different levels, joined by stairs and bordered by several handsome **patrician houses** of the 15C. The venerable Romanesque **Iglesia de San Martín★** (Church of St Martín) is surrounded on three sides by a gallery, with finely **carved capitals** on its columns.

Capilla de la Vera Cruz
(Chapel of the True Cross)
Situated outside the city walls north of the Alcázar, this 13C polygonal church was designed by the Knights Templar to reproduce Jerusalem's church of the Holy

The Casa de los Lozoya, with its 16C tower symbolising the owner's status, adjoins the medieval Plaza de San Martín.

Sepulchre. Belonging today to the Maltese
Order, it has a round nave for worshippers,
encircling a chapel originally containing a
piece of the True Cross – now in the nearby
village church of Zamarramala.

Other Attractions
Synagogue (Corpus Christi)
east of the cathedral
Now a convent church in Segovia's old
Jewish quarter.
Iglesia de San Esteban (St Stephen's Church)
Splendid 13C Romanesque church, with a
five-storey **tower**★ and porticoes with finely
sculpted capitals.
Riofrío★ 11km (6 miles) south of Segovia
The 18C palace of Isabella Farnese, wife of
Philip V, stands in a lovely oak forest. A
Museo de Caza (Hunting Museum) is
devoted to the king's favourite sport.

PALACIO DE LA GRANJA DE SAN ILDEFONSO★
To compensate for not getting the French
throne he so badly wanted, Philip V,
grandson of Louis XIV, built this opulent
baroque residence in the wooded hills
south-east of Segovia, where he could escape
from Madrid and the forbidding alternative
of El Escorial. He is buried in a chapel here
with his wife, Isabelle Farnese. The palace
halls include a richly endowed **Museo de
Tapices**★★ (Tapestry Museum).

French landscape architects and sculptors
have done fine work on the **Jardines**★★
(gardens), with formal gardens, topiary
hedges, **fountains**★★ and statuary, yet the
place derives its charm from the way the
Sierra de Guadarrama forests have
encroached to give the whole a most un-

French, more 'natural' touch of wilderness. Chestnut trees imported from France in the 18C have reached monumental proportions among the dense woods of local oak, elm, maple and poplar.

ÁVILA★★

An atmosphere of cheerful religious fervour reigns in the town. The home of St Teresa (1515–1582) attracts hundreds of pilgrims to her birthplace and the convents she founded, in particular busloads of Catholic schoolgirls whose teachers see in the great mystic a model for their faith. Against the growing trend in the Roman Catholic church towards a more relaxed attitude towards discipline in religious life, St Teresa reinforced the stricter observance of the Carmelite order.

Even the famous 11C **city walls★★**, still

Visitors can walk along the sentry path on top of Ávila's medieval city walls.

perfectly preserved in their embrace of the city, were initially an act of religious assertion. Alfonso VI had the granite ramparts, with their 90 towers, built by Muslim prisoners of war in 1093 after he had conquered the city for Christianity.

Catedral★★ (Cathedral)

Emphasizing the city's union of faith and force, the church's apse, with its crenellated outer wall, forms an integral part of the eastern fortifications. Begun in the 12C as a Romanesque church, Gothic and Renaissance features were added over the next 400 years. Inside, notice the fine **choir stalls**, two elegant wrought-iron **pulpits**, a monumental Renaissance **altar** in the apse by Pedro Berruguete and Giovanni da

Carvings over the entrance to the cathedral soften the rather austere exterior.

Bologna, and the elaborately carved **albaster tomb**★★ of Bishop Alonso de Madrigal, nicknamed **El Tostado**★★ (the Toasted One) for his swarthy complexion.

The Shrines of St Teresa

Built over the birthplace of Teresa de Cepeda y Ahumada on Plaza de la Santa, just inside the south city gate, is the **Convento de Santa Teresa (La Santa)**. Inside, you can visit the baroque church with a chapel marking the exact spot of the saint's birth, and paintings illustrating the miracles of her life. Next to the gift shop, a reliquary displays her rosary beads and one of her fingers. She was canonized in 1622 and declared a Doctor of the Church in 1970. Other pilgrimage shrines are outside the city walls:

The Convent of St Teresa was built over the site of the house where the saint was born.

north of the Parador Gate, **Convento de la Encarnación** (Incarnation Convent) in which she spent 30 years, first as a novice, then as prioress; east of the city centre, **Convento de San José (Las Madres)**, which she founded in 1562, the first of her 17 Carmelite convents; and on a rocky mound just west of town, **Cuatro Postes** (Four Posts) where the seven-year-old child was caught by her uncle after trying to run away with her brother, both seeking martyrdom at the hands of the Moors. This is a great spot from which to view the town, especially at sunset.

Other Attractions
Monasterio de Santo Tomás★
This Dominican monastery was expanded by the monarchs Isabella and Ferdinand in the late 15C as a summer residence. The tomb of Grand Inquisitor Torquemada lies in the sacristy.
Basílica de San Vicente★★
A huge Romanesque basilica with an ornate western porch. Inside is a 12C **tomb★★** of martyrs beneath a Gothic pagoda-shaped canopy.

ARANJUEZ★★
Like Spain's monarchs of old, many Madrileños head south in summer for the **Palacio Real★** (Royal Palace). After repeated fires, it has been renovated as a sparkling neo-classical summer residence. Among its showy splendours are the 18C rococo **Salón del Trono** (Throne Room) and the enchanting **Salón de Porcelana★★** (Porcelain Room), fashioned entirely in the porcelain factory of Madrid's Buen Retiro palace. The **Jardín del Príncipe★★** (the Prince's Garden) is a sprawling, shady, English-style

The Palacio Real, Aranjuez, seen from the lake.

landscaped park covering 150 hectares (370 acres) along the Tagus river. At the eastern end is the **Casa del Labrador★★** (the Labourer's Cottage), built in neo-classical style with sumptuous 18C decor.

CHINCHÓN★

This slice of Castilian village life is just 20km (13 miles) from Madrid. It is esteemed for its *anís* (aniseed liqueur) and, the people insist, the special qualities of its garlic. Centrepiece in every sense is the town's highly theatrical **Plaza Mayor★★** (Main Square). The two- and three-storey white stucco houses look down across wooden arcades at the oval plaza, alternating in summer as a stage for open-air plays and an arena for bullfights. Pride of the town's **church** is a Goya painting of *The Assumption*.

ENJOYING YOUR VISIT

WEATHER

Though that centuries-old adage about Madrid's 'nine months of winter and three months of hell' is grossly exaggerated, the continental climate in the middle of the peninsula does make for a very hot summer and bitterly cold winter. Ideally, April to June and September to October are the best times to go. If you must travel in July and August, follow the example of the Madrileños: wear light cottons and a good hat, and take frequent visits to the region's surrounding greenery. In the cold dry months from November to March, the dynamic spirit of *Movida* in the bars and theatres will keep you warm.

Enjoying a warm autumn day in Retiro Park.

CALENDAR OF EVENTS

In addition to national holidays (*see* p.122), there are a host of religious, sporting and cultural festivities in and around Madrid.

February
Carnaval (Carnival): Held the week before Shrove Tuesday, with costumed neighbourhood fiestas; Santa Águeda: (second weekend) in Segovia and the nearby village of Zamarramala, when women take over local government and medieval costumed processions take place.

March/April
Semana Santa (Holy Week): Festivities in Madrid and Segovia, with the most formal processions in Toledo; Passion Play in Chinchón.

2 May
Dos de Mayo: Week of celebrations of the 1808 insurrection, with concerts and dancing around Malasaña's Plaza Dos de Mayo.

15 May
Verbenas de San Isidro: Two weeks of festivals for Madrid's patron saint; bands, city parades, dancing in Jardines de las Vistillas.
Start of bullfight season at Las Ventas.

13 June
Fiesta de San Antonio de la Florida (St Anthony's Day): Festivities around the church.

24 June
Fiestas de San Juan: St John's summer solstice, saint's day for King Juan Carlos; bonfires and fireworks in Retiro Park; music and processions in Segovia.

July
Ávila Arts and Sports Festival.

9–16 July
Fiesta in Madrid's Chamberi neighbourhood (west of Castellana).

August
Virgen del Sagrario (Virgin of the Sanctuary): Fiesta in third week of the month in Toledo, culminating in spectacular fireworks.

15 August
Viergen de la Paloma (Virgin of the Dove): Festivities in Plaza de Paja in La Latina *barrio* and Las Vistillas gardens. Chinchón bull-runs through the streets.

September
Aranjuez concerts in palace gardens.

October
Festivales de Otoño: Autumn festival in Madrid, with theatre, opera, dance, concerts, circus, cinema and exhibitions. Feria de Santa Teresa: second week, Ávila festivities, market, concerts, bullfights, church organ recitals.

31 December
New Year's Eve: Big celebration on Puerta del Sol; good-luck grapes are eaten for each midnight chime.

Human statue in Plaza Mayor.

ACCOMMODATION

Accommodation in Madrid ranges from simple to luxurious, with prices to match. The *Michelin Red Guide España-Portugal* lists a selection of hotels. Prices do vary with demand, however, and while you can expect to pay more in high season, you will also be charged considerably more at times of popular feasts. Those travelling on their own also fare badly, as single rooms are in very short supply, and you may have to negotiate a reduced price for a double room.

Fondas (rooms) offer the most basic form of accommodation, and can be identified by a square blue sign with a white 'F' in it. They are often sited above a bar. Next come *casas de huéspedes* (CH on a similar background), *pensiones* (P, guesthouses), and *hospedajes*. More common than these four types of basic accommodation are *hostales* (marked Hs, hostels) and *hostal-residencias* (HsR, hostels with restaurant), both ranging from one to three stars and offering good en-suite or private facilities.

Hoteles (H) are graded from one to five stars, with a one-star hotel costing about the same as three-star *hostales*, but as you go up the scale the levels of luxury and pricing increase considerably.

State-run *paradores* are at the top of the scale, and these are often housed in beautiful restored historic castles, palaces and monasteries.

Details of youth hostels and other accommodation for students and young people are provided by TIVE, José Ortega y Gasset 71, 28006 Madrid; ☎ 347 7778. If you plan to take an extended trip out to the Guadarrama mountains, contact the Federación Española de Montañismo, Calle Alberto Aguilera 3, 28015 Madrid; ☎ 445 1382, who will provide you with information about *refugios*: basic dormitory huts offering cheap accommodation for hikers and climbers.

Recommended Accommodation

Madrid's better hotels are noted more for their modern facilities than for their romantic charm, but a few do stand out. Remember, when telephoning from abroad, dial 1 before the number. When calling from other parts of Spain dial 91 before the number.

Very Expensive (up to 49 000pts)

At the top end of the range are the Ritz and the Palace Hotel (*see* p.45), which will be beyond most people's budgets.

Expensive (20 000pts)

Gran Hotel Reina Victoria (*Plaza del Ángel 7*), with its colourful Bar Torero, is popular with bullfighters and *aficionados*.

Moderate (12 000-16 000pts)

Carlos V (*Maestro Vitoria 5* ☎ 531 4100)

The Palace Hotel offers luxury and old-fashioned elegance.

Comfortable hotel, pleasantly situated behind the Descalzas Reales Convent and within easy reach of Puerta del Sol.

NH Embajada (*Santa Engracia 5, Chamberí* ☎ 594 0213) Attractive building.

Moderno (*Arenal 2, Plaza Mayor/Puerta del Sol* ☎ 531 0900) Tourist hotel in the city centre.

Galiano Residencia (*Alcalá Galiano 6; near Plaza de Colón* ☎ 319 2000) Tastefully furnished stately mansion with comfortable spacious rooms; good value.

La Residencia de El Viso (*Nervión 8, Chamartín* ☎ 564 0370)

Inexpensive (6 000-11 000pts)

Near the Plaza Santa Ana area's lively *tapas* bars and restaurants, the reasonably-priced Gran Vía is the place for bargain *Hostal* boarding houses.

California (*Gran Vía 38* ☎ 522 4703)

Centro Sol (*Carrera de San Jerónimo 5, Puerta del Sol* ☎ 522 1582)

FOOD AND DRINK

Madrileños nurture the habit of starting meals so late (lunch is rarely before 2pm, while dinner is usually 9 or 10pm) by whetting their appetites with delicious little *tapas* (snacks). Connoisseurs make the rounds of several *tapas* bars (*tascas*) to try, with a glass of wine or beer, the speciality of each place. Don't try to beat them, join them – unless you prefer to eat in an empty restaurant or one that caters only to early-dining tourists. The décor and lively atmosphere in the *tasca* and other bars and taverns serving *tapas* is often so much more attractive than the conventional *restaurante* or *cafetería* that many end up making a whole meal of the appetizers.

Tapas

Hot or cold, and eaten with fingers or a toothpick, the snacks can be ordered either as a *porción* (single-helping), a larger *ración*, or *media-ración* (half-serving). Among the classics, which you can point to at the counter if you can't remember the Spanish word, are: fresh anchovies (*boquerones*), shrimp (*gambas*), squid (*calamares*), snails (*caracoles*), garlic mushrooms (*champiñones*), slice of potato omelette (*tortilla*), meatballs (*albóndigas*), olives (*aceitunas*), eggplant and pepper salad (*escalibada*), potato salad (*patatas alioli*) and spicy sautéed potatoes (*patatas bravas*).

A word about ham (*jamón*), a national obsession: all over Madrid, literally hundreds of dried hams can be seen hanging in windows of restaurants known as *Palacios* (palaces) or *Museos de jamón* (museums) of ham. The most popular, *Serrano*, is eaten in an open sandwich or by the plateful. Gourmets compare its merits with the prestigious *Jabugo* from Andalucía and Granada, and the *Montánchez* of Extremadura.

Main Dishes

Like many other capitals, Madrid offers in its wide range of restaurants a chance to taste regional cuisine from all over the country, often proposing its own distinctive versions of classic dishes.

Sopa de ajo (garlic soup) is a tangy peasant dish, but Madrid's variation has made it a delicacy – pieces of bread cooked in garlic, olive oil and hot peppers, with an egg added at the last minute to poach in the boiling hot broth.

Gazpacho is a chilled soup from Andalucía,

a refreshing summer favourite of liquefied tomatoes, chopped cucumber, green peppers, bread croûtons, olive oil and garlic.

Paella, named after the two-handled black frying pan in which the saffron rice is sautéed and mixed with chicken, originated in Valencia. It is now a national dish, found Mediterranean-coast style with shrimp, mussels and squid or, from Alicante, with rabbit and snails. It is a dish, strictly cooked to order, that Madrileños eat primarily for lunch.

Cocido madrileño is a delicious version of another national dish, presented in three servings: first the broth in which everything has been cooked, then the cabbage, potatoes, young turnips and chickpeas, and lastly the beef, marrow-bone, pork, *chorizo* sausage and black pudding.

On your excursions, try the great Castillian

A typical meal of paella.

speciality, *cochinillo asado* or *Tostón* (roast suckling pig), at its tenderest best in Segovia, as is the *cordero asado* (roast lamb). Besides the humble, but succulent *carcamusa* (meat-stew), Toledo is reputed for game birds, particularly its red partridge, pheasant and quail.

Cheese and Desserts

Spain's most admired cheese is La Mancha's *queso manchego*, made from ewe's milk; it comes either dry and sharp or creamy and mild. Desserts (*postres*) include *arroz con leche* (rice pudding), *flan* (caramel custard) and Madrileño pastries known as *rosquillas tontas y listas* (ring-cakes with aniseed and sugar). Toledo produces delicious *mazapán* (almond marzipan), a Moorish legacy, and Ávila is famous for its *yemas de Santa Teresa* (candied egg-yolk).

Bar, with typical coloured tiled wall murals.

Wines

To most Madrileños, *vino* just means red
wine. To be more specific, they may say *tinto*
(full-bodied) or *clarete* (light red), more
rarely *blanco* (white), from Galicia or
Aragón. The most prestigious reds are *Rioja*,
from the Ebro Valley in northern Spain.
Madrid's table wine (*vino de la casa*) is more
likely to be La Mancha's *Valdepeñas*, which
are generally lighter and slightly acidic.

As an apéritif, sherry from Jerez de la
Frontera in Andalucía is served dry (*fino* or
seco) or medium (*amontillado*), and as a
dessert wine, dark and sweet (*oloroso*). The
cool summer drink, *sangría*, is a punch of
red wine, brandy, orange and lemon juice,
mineral water, ice and sliced fruit.

Recommendations: Tapas Bars

Since so many people find tapas a meal in
itself, we first propose a few of our favourite
tapas bars.

In the area of Plaza Mayor – Puerta del Sol
Historic **Casa Labra** (*Calle de Tetuán*), where
the Spanish Socialist Party was founded in
1879; delicious fried cod.

On and off Plaza de Santa Ana – Huertas
The old-fashioned beer-house and former
Hemingway hang-out, **Cervecería Alemana**
(right on the plaza), is expensive but
pleasant; the beautifully tiled bar of **Los
Gabrieles** (*Calle Echegaray*) serves modest
tapas but fine drinks; **Taberna de Dolores**
(*Plaza de Jesús 4*) is a charming early 20C bar,
whose façade is decorated with azulejos.

Around El Rastro
Try the bustling **Barranco** (*San Isidro
Labrador 14*) for its excellent shrimp
(*gambas*); **Los Caracoles** (*Plaza Cascorro 18*)
serves good snails and other tasty snacks.

Recommendations: Restaurants

With Madrid renewing its telephone system, some of these numbers may be changing; check with hotel reception before calling. Here are a few suggestions, but more complete listings are available in the *Michelin Red Guide España-Portugal*.

In the area of Plaza Mayor – Puerta del Sol

Casa Ciriaco (*Calle Mayor 84* ☎ 548 0620) Historic restaurant once frequented by artists and literati (moderate).

Café de Chinitas (*Calle Torija 7* ☎ 547 1502) offers authentic flamenco with traditional Madrid cooking (moderate to expensive).

Las Cuevas de Luis Candelas (*Cuchilleros 1*

Call in for a drink and to enjoy the elegant tiled bar at Los Gabrieles.

☎ 366 5428) Staff dressed in the costume of ancient highwaymen serve you in this traditionally decorated restaurant (expensive).

Botín (*Calle Chuchilleros 17* ☎ 366 4217) Historic tavern popular with tourists.

La Bola (*Bola 5* ☎ 547 6930) Popular taberna specializing in *cocido* (moderate).

El Asador de Aranda (at three locations: *Preciados 44, Puerta del Sol,* ☎ 547 2156; *Diego de León 9, Salamanca* ☎ 563 0246, *Plaza de Castilla 3, Chamartín* ☎ 733 8702) Castillan decor; roast lamb a speciality (moderate to expensive).

Around Plaza de Santa Ana – Huertas
Champagneria Gala (*Calle Moratín 22,* ☎ 429 2562) Pleasant decor with garden patio; speciality paella (inexpensive).

Domine Cabra (*Calle Huertas 54* ☎ 429 4365), where inventive efforts to update lusty traditional dishes for more refined tastes are made (moderate).

Plaza de España
La Rioja (*Las Negras 8* ☎ 548 0497) Medieval decor (moderate).

Salamanca
La Trainera (*Calle Lagasca 60* ☎ 576 0575) One of Madrid's most popular seafood restaurants, with an informal atmosphere (expensive).

La Giralda IV (*Claudio Coello 24* ☎ 576 4069) Andalusían decor and cuisine (expensive).

Parque del Oeste
Casa Mingo (*Paseo de la Florida 2* ☎ 547 7918) Traditional Asturian cuisine (roasted chicken and cider); a favourite haunt of students; outdoor dining (inexpensive).

Around Rastro
Malacatín (*Calle de la Ruda 3* ☎ 365 5241) Rustic tavern serving traditional hearty fare such as *cocido* (moderate).

SHOPPING

The *Movida* of the 1980s has breathed new life into Madrid's shops. Fashion for women and men is innovative, challenging the French and Italian 'establishment' with its freer spirit. In addition, a revival in traditional craftsmanship offers tourists a quality alternative to the tired old souvenir trade.

The city's main shopping area is along Gran Vía and around Puerta del Sol, where the **department store** El Corte Inglés has its flagship store. Besides the clothes of many of Spain's top fashion designers, these stores offer the shopper in a hurry a fair selection of handicraft goods. More offbeat and avant-garde shops can be found on Chueca's Calle Almirante and in the Malasaña neighbourhood.

Madrid has plenty to offer keen shoppers.

Clothes

Calle Serrano is one of Madrid's main fashion streets, with Loewe at nos 26 and 34, and the classic clothes of Adolfo Domínguez at no 96 (for men *Calle Ortega y Gasset, 4*). One of Spain's leading designers for women is Sybilla (*Calle Jorge Juan 12*), but prices are high. Her work is also sold at the avant-garde shop, Ekseption (*Calle Velázquez 28*). Two highly creative, more reasonably priced Chueca stores are Blackmarket (*Calle Colón 3*), for women's clothes, and Excrupulus Net (*Calle Almirante 7*) selling Spanish designer **shoes** for men and women. Alpargatería Lobo (*Calle Toledo 30*) specializes in **espadrilles** (*alpargatas*) in an amazing range of different colours.

For traditional **hats**, caps and berets, Madrid's oldest hatshop is Casa Yustas (*Plaza Mayor 30*).

These colourful Spanish fans make lovely gifts and souvenirs.

Crafts

The best all-round centre is El Arco de Los Cuchilleros (*Plaza Mayor 9*). Serving as an outlet for more than 20 modern and traditional workshops from all over the country, it sells embroidered goods, textiles, jewellery, leather, wooden games and ceramics. One of the city's leading **guitar** specialists, but expensive, is José Ramírez (*Calle Concepción Jerónima*). For **toys**, try Puck (*Calle Duque de Sesto 30*). The specialist in ladies' **fans** is Casa Jiménez (*Calle Preciados 42*).

ENTERTAINMENT AND NIGHTLIFE

There is more to Madrid's nightlife than **discos** (*discotecas* and *discobares*) but even if that *was* all, they alone could keep you up all night every night for a year – and you wouldn't need to go to the same place twice.

Start off the evening with a drink at one of the pavement cafés.

There are literally hundreds all over the city and suburbs, but most of them are on and around the city centre's Gran Vía, Puerta del Sol and Plaza de Santa Ana and in the neighbourhoods of Chueca and Malasaña.

Flamenco in Madrid has undergone the same modernizing influences as the rest of Spanish culture since the 1980s. To the insistent throb of the guitars, stamping heels, snapping fingers and heartfelt passionate song of the traditional form, perhaps of Arabic origin, has been added the new music of modern jazz and rock. The *nuevo flamenco* (new flamenco) can be heard

A visit to Madrid is not complete without experiencing the passion of traditional flamenco.

at the Revolver Club (*Calle Galileo 26*). The more traditional flamenco, alternating between the bouncy, cheerful songs known as *cante chico* and the sorrowful, heart-rending dirges of *cante jondo*, is performed at La Soleo (*Cava Baja 27*) and the historic Candela (*Calle del Olmo 2*).

Opera is more seriously back in business as the Teatro Real re-opens its doors, after lengthy renovation and **classical music** concerts are held at the Auditorio Nacional de Música, home of the Spanish National Orchestra (*Orquesta Nacional de España*).

And every night-owl's last stop, whether rock fan or opera buff, seems to be the Chocolatería San Ginés, Pasadizo de San Ginés, near the Teatro Real. Since 1894, it has been serving hot chocolate and those sweet fried dough sticks known as *churros* before people head, at last, for bed.

SPORTS

There seem to be only two sports that really matter to Madrileños – **bullfighting** and **football**. Despite growing opposition inside Spain to the annual killing of 24 000 bulls nationwide, *aficionados* still make their way to Madrid's Plaza Monumental de Las Ventas, high temple of the national sport. The season is launched in May with two weeks of bullfights to celebrate the city's patron saint, San Isidro. Thereafter, the ritual of sun, blood and sudden death is played out every Sunday afternoon.

Football fans insist that this antique passion is overshadowed today by the joy and misery under the sun or floodlights of Real Madrid's Santiago Bernabeu Stadium, or at Atlético Madrid's Vicente Calderón. Here, defeat is as bitter as death, but less bloody.

The packed stadium at Las Ventas is testament to the popularity of bullfighting in Madrid.

THE BASICS

Before You Go

Visitors entering Spain should be in possession of a valid passport. No visa is required for members of EU countries or US, Canadian or New Zealand citizens, but visitors from Australia do require a visa, which can be obtained on arrival for a period of up to 30 days. No vaccinations are necessary.

Getting There

By Air: Most international airlines have flights to Barajas Airport, 16km (10 miles) east of Madrid.

There are numerous scheduled flights to Spain. Visitors coming from the US will probably fly direct to Madrid, though sometimes it is cheaper to fly to London or another European city first, then get a connecting flight to Spain. The superfast trains – the AVE and the Talgo – connect Madrid with Córdoba (2½ hours), Seville (3 hours) and Málaga (3-4 hours).

Scheduled flights leave all year round for Madrid from Dublin and Belfast.

Visitors from Australia and New Zealand cannot get a direct flight to Spain, and will have to make a stopover at another European city.

Low-cost flights from anywhere in the world can be arranged through flight agents or by booking a charter flight. These usually offer the best price deal, but return flights are fixed so that the maximum time you can spend in Spain is four weeks. Package holidays offer great value too, and sometimes the price is so reasonable that you can buy a holiday to a resort where you would not wish to stay, and still afford to stay in the place of your choice.

Apex or super-apex tickets may be bought directly from the airlines. The travel ads in the English Sunday papers or the various London listing magazines are the best places for travellers from the UK to look. Travel clubs and discount agents offer good savings from North America and Australasia.

By Coach: Coaches leave London for Madrid several times a week, and journey times are tediously long, so a stopover inside the Spanish border is recommended.

By Train: Le Shuttle takes cars under the English Channel from Folkestone in 35 minutes. A connection can be made at Paris with the Expresso Puerta del Sol, which leaves each night for Spain. Pedestrians an take the Eurostar from ondon through the Channel unnel, and must then change ain stations in Paris (Gare du ord to Austerlitz) to catch the algo Camas/ Couchette, hich also leaves nightly.

There are various rail passes hich offer substantial iscounts on rail travel, partic- larly if you are planning to avel within Europe. Details e obtainable from Rail urope in New York (☎ 800 38 7245), or Eurotrain in ondon (☎ 0171 730 3402), r British Rail European formation (☎ 0171 834 345).

There are various options or those wanting to take their vn car to Southern Spain.

By Ferry: Two ferries companies offer direct sailings to Bilbao and Santander from Britain: Brittany Ferries and P&O European Ferries. The advantage of this crossing is that the long – and expensive – drive through France is com- pletely eliminated.

Several ferry companies carry cars and passengers across the Channel, with the quickest journeys being between Dover/Calais, and Folkestone/Boulogne. The hovercraft is even faster, crossing from Dover to Calais in just 35 minutes. Brittany Ferries offer crossings from Portsmouth, Plymouth and Poole directly to Brittany, arriving at St Malo and Roscoff.

ocha train station, with its tropical gardens.

A-Z

Accidents and Breakdowns

If you are involved in an accident while driving in Spain you should exchange full details of insurance, addresses, etc. In an emergency, if you can find a telephone dial 091 *See also* **Driving**.

Accommodation *see* p.94

Airports *see* **Getting There** p.110

Babysitters *see* **Children**

Banks

Banks are open 8.30/9am-2pm, Monday to Friday. Main branches are also open on Saturday from 9am-12.30/1pm. Between June and September most banks are closed on Saturdays.

Most major credit cards are accepted by hotels and department stores. Girobank operates an international cash card system which allows cash withdrawals on personal UK bank accounts. For details of

Delta Card contact Girobank Bootle, Merseyside, GIR OAA ☎ 01645 250 250.

Eurocheques backed up by Eurocheque card can be used in banks, and to pay for goods in hotels, restaurants and shops. Most cheque cards, and Visa and Mastercard, can be used to withdraw cash from automatic cash machines.

Banks will usually change travellers' cheques, but charge high commission rates, and there are also specialist exchange bureaux. Exchange facilities at El Corte Inglés, a department store found throughout Spain, offer competitive rates.

Bicycles

Cycling is a cheap way of getting about in Spain, but the hair-raising traffic in Madrid makes it inadvisable here. A short cycling trip out to the surrounding countryside can make a pleasant outing, but the terraine is rather too monotonous for an extended cycle tour. There are several bike shops, and garages also sometimes carry bike spares.

Most airlines will take bicycles as ordinary baggage, although chartered flights may not have sufficient space. Bikes can travel in the guard's van on suburban trains only.

Breakdowns see **Accidents**

Buses see **Transport**

Camping

There are several good campsites situated just outside Madrid. For a free list of these sites, contact the Spanish National Tourist Office in your own country, or obtain one locally from any tourist office (see **Tourist Information Offices**).

Unauthorized camping is not recommended, and though you might just get moved on by the authorities, you may be unlucky.

For particular information on campsites or making a booking, contact the site directly, or Federación Española de Empresarios de Campings y CV General Oraa, 52-2°D 28006 Madrid; ☎ 562 9994.

Car Hire

Car hire companies are based in the city centre as well as at Barajas Airport. Airlines and tour operators offer fly/drive arrangements, which can be very good value. Make sure that collision damage waiver is included in the insurance. Automatics should be reserved in advance and are more expensive.

The lower age limit is 21, but few international companies hire to drivers under 23, or even 25. Drivers must have held their full licence for at least a year.

With the exception of Avis, there is an upper age limit of 60-65. Unless paying by credit card a substantial cash deposit is usually required. If you are driving a car that has obviously been hired, take extra precautions when parking it to deter thieves, and never leave anything of value inside.

See also **Accidents and Breakdowns** and **Tourist Information Offices**

Spanish guitarist.

Children

Children are welcomed in Spain, and hotel owners are usually happy to offer rooms with three or four beds to accommodate families. Babysitting services are generally available, or in smaller, family-run hotels the owners will often listen out for problems while you are out.

Baby food and disposable nappies can be bought from supermarkets and chemists, but you might want to bring your own powdered milk, as the Spanish type is heat-treated.

Children under three can travel free on trains, and those under seven are charged only half price.

Churches see Religion

Climate see p. 92

Climate see p. 92

Clothing

The Madrileños are fairly liberal in their attitudes to dress, although they are very keen on looking smart and tidy at all times. In the evenings, in particular, they make a great effort; men often wear a suit for a night out clubbing. Beachwear is frowned upon, although mini-skirts and shorts are quite acceptable; places of worship and museums will often exclude those who are not dressed appropriately. Hats are a good idea at the height of summer, particularly in the early afternoon.

See also **Etiquette**

Complaints

Complaints about goods or services should ideally be made at the time. At a hotel or restaurant make your complaint in a calm manner to the manager.

All hotels, restaurants, camp sites and petrol stations are required by law to keep and produce complaint forms when requested by a customer. If this proves difficult, ask the local tourist information office to intervene on your behalf (*see* **Tourist Information Offices**).

Consulates see Embassies

Crime

Being the victim of petty crime – commonly pick-pocketing and bag-snatching – can ruin a holiday, so take every precaution to prevent this happening to you. The best advice is to be aware at all times, carry as little money, and as few credit cards as possible, and leave any valuables in the hotel safe.

Carry wallets and purses in secure pockets, wear body belts

or carry handbags across your body or firmly under your arm. Never leave your car unlocked, as this is an open invitation to thieves. Also make sure that you never leave any valuables or luggage in the car, even when it is parked in an apparently secure car park. If you have to leave things in the car, ensure they are well hidden. Hire cars in particular are targeted by thieves, and if possible you should remove any evidence that your car has been hired.

If you have anything stolen, report it immediately to the nearest police station or police office – Centro Atención Policial – where English-speaking officers can offer practical advice. Collect a report so that you can make an insurance claim.

If your passport is stolen, report it to your Embassy at once.

The Crystal Palace, Retiro Park.

Currency see **Money**

Customs and Entry Regulations

There is no limit on the importation into Spain of tax-paid goods bought in an EU country, provided they are for personal consumption, with the exception of alcohol and tobacco which have fixed limits governing them.

Disabled Visitors

Spain is not the most accessible country for disabled travellers, and public transport is particularly difficult for wheelchair users. The *Michelin Red Guide España-Portugal* indicates which hotels have facilities for the disabled.

In Britain, RADAR, at 12 City Forum, 250 City Road, London EC1V 8AF; ☎ 0171 250 3222, publish fact sheets, as well as an annual guide to facilities and accommodation overseas.

The Spanish National Tourist Office in your own country is a good source of advance information, and you are also advised to check with hotels and travel carriers to see that your individual needs can be met.

Driving

Drivers should carry a full national or preferably international driving licence, insurance documents including a green card (no longer compulsory for EU members but strongly recommended), registration papers for the car, and a nationality sticker for the car rear.

A bail bond or extra insurance cover for legal costs is also worth investing in. Without a bail bond the car could be impounded and the driver placed under arrest.

The minimum age for driving is 18, and cars drive on the right. Away from main roads cars give way to those approaching from the right. Front seat passengers must wear seatbelts outside of urban areas.

Speed traps are used, and if you are caught, the police are likely to impose a hefty fine.

Speed limits are as follows:
• Maximum on urban roads: 60kph/37mph
• Maximum on other roads: 90kph or 100kph/56 or 62mph
• Dual carriageways: 120kph/75mph.

Also note that Spanish motorways have tolls.

Dry Cleaning see **Laundry**

Electric Current

The voltage in Spain is usually 220 or 225V. Plugs and sockets are of the two-pin variety, and daptors are generally required. North Americans will probably lso need a transformer.

Embassies

American Embassy
Serrano 175,
28006 Madrid
☎ 557 40 00

Australian Embassy
Paseo de la Castellana 143,
28046 Madrid
☎ 579 04 28

British Embassy
Calle Fernando el Santo 16,
28010 Madrid
☎ 319 02 00

Canadian Embassy
Calle Núñez de Balboa 35,
28001 Madrid
☎ 431 43 00

Embassy of Ireland
Claudio Coello 73,
28001 Madrid
☎ 576 35 00

Emergencies

In an emergency, either go to the police or contact your embassy, who will offer very limited help. The universal emergency telephone number is ☎ 091.

Etiquette

As in most places in the world, it is considered polite and respectful to cover up decently in churches and museums. Be sensitive to conservative attitudes outside the city, and don't upset the locals by dressing provocatively or otherwise showing a lack of respect.

Excursions

For details of excursions and trips which can easily be made from Madrid, *see* pp.70-91. Information on excursions and attractions can be obtained from the local tourist information office or your travel agency.

Guidebooks *see* **Maps**

Health

UK nationals should carry a

Tiled street sign.

Form E111 which is produced by the Department of Health, and which entitles the holder to free urgent treatment for accident or illness in EU countries (forms are available from post offices). The treatment will have to be paid for in the first instance, but the money can be reclaimed later. All foreign nationals, including those from the UK, are advised to take out comprehensive insurance cover, and to keep any bills, receipts and invoices to support any claim.

Lists of doctors can be obtained from hotels, chemists and embassies, and first aid and medical advice is also available at the *farmacia*, from pharmacists who are highly trained and can dispense drugs which are available only on prescription in other countries.

The *farmacia* is generally open at 9.30/10am, close for lunch at 1.30/2pm and then reopen at 4.30/5pm till around 8pm. Some are open for longer; those which are open late or on Sundays display notices on their doors, and on the doors of other pharmacies.

You can get the address of an English-speaking doctor from your consulate, the police station, the *farmacia* or the tourist office.

Hours *see* **Opening Hours**

Information *see* **Tourist Information Offices**

Language
Most Madrileños speak some English, but are not generally pleased by tourists who make no effort to speak Spanish; even a few simple words and phrases will often be warmly received. In out of town areas very little English is spoken, and it is advisable, at the very least, to carry a phrase book.

Opposite are a few words and phrases that will help you make the most of your stay in Madrid.

Laundry
Self-service launderettes (*lavanderías*) exist, but are rare. More common are the service laundries where you are charged for someone else to do the work. For dry cleaning look for the sign *tintorería*.

Lost Property
Spanish airports and major railway stations have their own lost property offices. If something is missing in your hotel, check first with the front desk and hotel security. Report all lost or stolen items to the police, and always make sure to get a report to substantiate any

Yes/no / Sí/no

Please/thank you / Por favor/gracias

Do you speak English? / ¿Habla (usted) inglés?

How much is it? / ¿Cuánto es?

Excuse me / Perdone

I'd like a stamp / Quisiera un sello

How are you? / ¿Cómo está (usted)?

I don't understand / No entiendo

See you later / Hasta luego

Do you have a room? / ¿Tiene una habitación?

How do I get to ...? / ¿Por dónde se va a ...?

---

insurance claims, but do not expect the police to get too excited about minor thefts.

Should you lose any travel documents, contact the police, and in the event of a passport going missing, inform your Embassy or Consulate immediately (*see* **Embassies**).

Lost or stolen travellers' cheques and credit cards should be reported immediately to the issuing company with a list of numbers, and the police should also be informed.

Maps

There is a range of Michelin road atlases and sheet maps of Madrid and the surrounding area. The *Michelin Map 40 Madrid* covers the city, with a useful street index. The *Michelin Green Guide Spain* contains useful information on the sights and attractions in Madrid and also describes many of the towns and villages surrounding the city which you may be interested in visiting. The *Michelin Red Guide España/Portugal* lists accommodation and restaurants.

The spiral-bound *Michelin Road Atlas: Spain and Portugal* covers the whole of the Iberian peninsula, *Michelin Map 990* covers the whole of Spain, while *Maps 442-445* include Madrid and the surrounding areas and are useful for excursions around Madrid and for route-planning.

Hiking maps can be ordered from: Servicio de Publicaciones

del Instituto Geográfico Nacional, General Ibáñez de Ibero 3, 28003, Madrid. Book-shops, street kiosks and petrol stations offer a good selection of maps for sale.

Medical Care *see* Health

Money

The Spanish unit of currency is the peseta, with notes in denominations of 1 000, 2 000, 5 000 and 10 000 pesetas, and coins of 1, 5, 10, 25, 50, 100, 200 and 500 pesetas.

There is no restriction on bringing into or out of the country currency below the level of one million pesetas, but perhaps the safest way to carry large amounts of money is in travellers' cheques, which are widely accepted. Exchange counters are found at airports, terminals and larger railway stations, at the El Corte Inglés department stores and at banks (*see* **Banks**).

Lost or stolen travellers' cheques and credit cards should be reported immed-

Fruit shop.

ately to the issuing company
with a list of numbers, and the
police should also be informed.

Newspapers

There are several Spanish daily
papers sold in Madrid,
including *El País*, *El Mundo*,
ABC and *Diario 16*. *El Mundo*
and *El País* have useful entertainment listings supplements
on Fridays, and *ABC* has one
on Thursdays.

If you are looking for
English language media,
Lookout and *In Spain* are both
monthly magazines, produced
primarily for the English-
speaking ex-pat community.
British and other foreign
newspapers are widely
available, and the *International
Herald Tribune*, published in
Paris, offers the latest stock
market news from America as
well as world news.

Opening Hours

Shops in Madrid normally open
9.30-10am, close for lunch
from 1.30/2pm, and then
reopen at 4.30/5pm. They stay
open till 8pm, or sometimes
later in the summer.

Chemists *(farmacia)* are usually
open the same hours as shops
(see above), but some are
open for longer and on
Sundays, and some stay open
late, or even 24 hours. These

are marked by a sign in the
window, and other pharmacies
also carry details. Call ☎ 098
for comprehensive information.
Monuments and museums
tend to open between 10am-
1pm and 4-7pm, with several
variations, while many
churches only open for the
early morning or evening
service each day.
See also **Banks** *and* **Post Offices**

Photography

Good-quality film and camera
equipment are available in
Madrid, and facilities for fast
processing are plentiful,
although this is often
expensive.

Before taking photographs
in museums and art galleries it
is wise to check with staff as
photography is usually
restricted in these places.

Police

There are three types of police:
the Guardia Civil, who wear
green uniforms; the Policía
Municipal, who wear blue and
white uniforms with red trim
and are generally sympathetic to
tourists with genuine problems;
and the Policía Nacional, who
wear dark blue uniforms.

The national emergency
telephone number is ☎ 091;
the local emergency telephone
number is ☎ 092.

Post Offices

Madrid's main post office (*Correos*), in the Plaza de Cibeles, is open from 9am-8pm. It gets very busy at times, so if you only want to buy stamps, it is a good idea to buy them from a tobacconist (*estanco*).

Poste restante mail should be sent to the person (surname underlined) at Lista de Correos, followed by the name of the town and province. Take a passport along as proof of identity when collecting mail. British visitors can withdraw cash on their UK accounts with a National Giro-bank postcheque (*see* **Banks**).

Public Holidays

New Year's Day: 1 January
Epiphany: 6 January
Good Friday to Easter Monday
Labour Day: 1 May
Corpus Christi: 2nd Thursday
    after Whitsun
Assumption Day: 15 August
National Day: 12 October
All Saints' Day: 1 November
Constitution Day: 6 December
Immaculate Conception:
    8 December
Christmas Day: 25 December
    There are also other feasts and public holidays which are celebrated locally, when almost everything shuts down:
Comunidad de Madrid: 2 May
San Isidro: 15 May

Public Transport
see **Transport**

Religion

Spain is a Catholic country, and there are daily services in the churches and cathedrals. The location of churches and the times of services are best checked locally.
See **Tourist Information Offices**

Smoking

Legislation protects the rights of non-smokers over those of smokers in Spain these days, and smoking is banned in many public places. Signs in department stores, cinemas and public transport indicating that smoking is banned should be strictly adhered to.

Stamps *see* **Post Offices**

Taxis *see* **Transport**

Telephones

International telephone calls may be made from all Spanish provincial capital towns and most of the major holiday resorts. Dial 07, wait for the dialling tone, and then dial the appropriate country code (44 for the UK, 353 for Eire, 1 for USA and Canada, 61 for Australia and 64 for New Zealand).

Spanish telephones have instructions in English, and take 5, 25 or 100 peseta coins, or phonecards of 1 000 or 2 000 pesetas which can be bought at tobacconists (estancos). International calls may be made in either telephone booths, or at a Telefónica office where you pay after the call.

For calls within Spain, dial 9 followed by the area code. When telephoning Madrid from elsewhere in Spain, dial 1 before the number. Drop the 9 when dialing from abroad. The number for Directory Enquiries is 003, area codes 009, International Operator 008 for Europe and 005 for the rest of the world.

As in most countries, telephone calls made from hotels may be more straightforward and convenient, but they are more expensive.

Time difference

Spanish standard time is GMT plus one hour. Spanish summer time begins on the last Sunday in March at 2am when the clocks go forward an hour (the same day as British Summer Time), and it ends on the last Sunday in October at 3am when the clocks go back again.

Tipping

In Spain it is usual to tip between 5-10 per cent of the bill at bars, cafés and restau-

Shopping for souvenirs in Segovia.

rants, even though bills already include a service charge. The tip is related to customer satisfaction so the amount can vary each time. Porters, doormen, taxi drivers and cinema usherettes all expect a financial token of appreciation.

Toilets

There are many names for toilets in Spain, so look out for the following: *baños* (bathrooms), *aseos*, *servicios*, *sanitarios*, *damas* (ladies) or *caballeros* (gentlemen), *señoras* (women) or *señores* (men).

Tourist Information Offices

The Spanish National Tourist Office is an excellent first source of information for your holiday, on everything from where to stay to where and when the lesser known fiestas are held. Offices can be found at the following addresses:

UK
57-58 St James's Street,
London SW1A 1LD
☎ (0171) 499 0901
Canada
102 Bloor Street West,
14th Floor, Toronto,
Ontario M5S 1M8
☎ (416) 961 3131
Australia
203 Castlereagh Street,
Suite 21a, PO Box A685,

Sydney, NSW
☎ (02) 264 7966
USA
665 Fifth Avenue,
New York, NY10022
☎ (212) 759 8822, and
Water Tower Place,
Suite 915 East,
845 North Michigan Avenue,
Chicago, IL 60611
☎ (312) 642 1992

Tourist information centres which can be found in most large towns throughout Spain, are well stocked with leaflets providing information on excursions, transport, entertainment, facilities for the disabled, and exhibitions, as well as accommodation and restaurants. Guide books and maps are also for sale.

Madrid's *Oficinas de Turismo*, usually known simply as *turismo*, can be found at:
Aeropuerto de Barajas
☎ 3 05 86 56
Duque de Medinaceli 2
☎ 4 29 59 51
Estación de Chamartín
☎ 3 15 99 76
Oficina Municipal de información, Plaza Mayor 3
☎ 366 5477
Torre de Madrid, Plaza de España
☎ 5 41 23 25

Tours see Excursions

Transport

Madrid has an excellent **Metro** service, although it is one of the oldest in Europe. It has 115 stations and operates between 5.30am-1.30am. The system is easy to follow and is generally efficient, although rush hours (between 8.30-9.30am, 1.30-2.30pm and 8-9pm) are extremely hectic, and the lack of air conditioning makes these times almost unbearable in the summer. Prices are reasonable, and there are various discounts available.

Madrid's **buses** run between 6am-12pm, and a special nightbus leaves every hour on the hour from Cibeles and the Puerta del Sol. A ticket costs 90 pesetas, regardless of the length of your journey. A 10-journey bus-pass known as a *Bonobus*, costing 410 pesetas, may be purchased from outlets all over Madrid, including bus information kiosks, newspaper stalls and tobacconists, and the Caja de Madrid bank.

An *Abono* costs 3 000 pesetas (2 000 for children and 1 000 for senior citizens) and covers you for a full month of unlimited journeys around Madrid. The main drawback is Madrid's terrible traffic.

Taxis are a fairly economical alternative form of transport. Although they also suffer

The impressive home stadium of Madrid's main football team, Real Madrid.

delays from the traffic, they are more able to dodge the trouble-spots, and are obviously more direct than buses. They are painted white with a diagonal red stripe along the side and bear the Madrid City emblem on the rear doors. When available they show a green *libre* sign, and a green light at night.

Fares vary depending on various factors. Drivers should have a list of approved charges for the different runs, and will quote on request before you set off. On top of the basic charge, there is a surcharge for night time, weekends and public holidays, and also for pick-ups and drop-offs at certain parts of the city. The driver is permitted to start charging double the amount shown on the meter as soon as he crosses the city boundaries into the suburbs, so trains are the best option for transport out of Madrid.

Trains from out of town areas may be caught from Chamartín, Nuevos Ministe-rios, Recoletos, Atocha and Príncipe Pío/Norte stations, all of which are connected to the metro system. For details of discounts on train fares enquire at Spanish Railways RENFE, or a tourist office in your own country or in Madrid.
See **Tourist Information Offices** *and* **Driving**

TV and Radio

TVE 1 and TVE 2 are Spain's two nationwide television channels. Madrid also has Antena 3, Tele 5 and Tele-madrid.

The choice is a mixture of good live sports coverage, game shows, dubbed foreign language films and series, and soap operas from the US, Australia, the UK and South America.

English radio programmes may be picked up on the BBC World Service on short-wave radio, as well as on the Torrejón American Airforce Base station at 100.2 FM.

Vaccinations
see **Before You Go p.110**

Water

Madrid's water is safe to drink though most people prefer to drink the bottled variety.

Youth Hostels
see **Accommodation**

INDEX